**A New Library of
the Supernatural**

The Cosmic Influence

the Cosmic Influence

by Francis King

Doubleday and Company, Inc. Garden City, New York, 1976

EDITORIAL CONSULTANTS:

COLIN WILSON
DR. CHRISTOPHER EVANS

Series Coordinator: John Mason
Design Director: Günter Radtke
Picture Editor: Peter Cook
Editor: Mary Senechal
Copy Editor: Mitzi Bales
Research: Sarah Waters
General Consultant: Beppie Harrison

Library of Congress Cataloging in Publication Data
King, Francis
The Cosmic Influence
(A New Library of the Supernatural)
1. Astrology I. Title II. Series
BF1708.1.K57   133.5   76-5699
ISBN 0-385-11314-5

Doubleday and Company
ISBN: 0-385-11314-5
Library of Congress Catalog
Card No. 76-5699
A New Library of the Supernatural
ISBN: 11327-7
© 1976 Aldus Books Limited, London
D. L.: S.S.: 317/76
Printed and bound in Spain
by TONSA San Sebastián

Frontispiece: the Lagoon nebula in Sagittarius.
Above: the zodiac in May, from a medieval calendar.

The Cosmic Influence

The possibility of reading futures in the stars has long fascinated men. The science—or art—of astrology has had devoted followers since the time of the Babylonians, and never more than now. Is there a place for astrology in our rational world? What is our relationship to the stars? Is astrology, in fact, for real?

Contents

1 The Queen of Sciences   6
The development and honored position of astrology as one of the earliest sciences.

2 Astrology is For Real   28
Today's scientists are looking at principles of astrology and finding verification.

3 The Power of Prediction   46
The curious history of astrology in World War II and its influence on the Nazi top leaders.

4 Earth in Chaos   62
The idea that the cosmos in historical time wrought havoc upon the Earth.

5 The Zodiac and You   76
The signs of the zodiac and characteristics of those subject to their influence.

6 Your Personal Star Chart   108
How to go about constructing your own horoscope.

7 Interpreting Your Chart   124
Understanding what your horoscope reveals about your personality and possibilities.

8 Astrology Today   142
What is the true significance of the Queen of Sciences for men and women of today?

1

The Queen of Sciences

On February 24, 1975, members of royal families and leading statesmen from all over the world gathered in Nepal to attend the coronation of the country's new king. It was an elaborate and glittering ceremony, filmed for millions of television viewers across the globe. In accordance with Eastern custom, the date of the coronation had been chosen by Nepal's astrologers. King, government, and country had awaited their choice of a favorable date.

The leaders of Nepal are by no means the only Asian rulers of modern times to adhere to traditional oriental astrology. In both Burma and Sri Lanka, formerly Ceylon, new

Above: Ingrid Lind, a modern astrologer, with an astrological chart. Most of the 20th-century astrologers have preferred to shed the aura of mystery in an effort to make astrology accepted by and accessible to the ordinary person. A modern astrologer generally wishes to be regarded like any other professional, whose art lies in interpretation of a science.

"Millions of horoscopes are cast every year in the United States alone"

governments take office at the exact times worked out as propitious by official astrologers. In Sikkim, a province of northern India, the then Crown Prince married his American bride in March 1963 after waiting a year for astrologers to choose their wedding day. Pandit Jawaharlal Nehru, one of the founders of modern India and his country's prime minister for 14 years, was a firm believer in astrology. When his first grandson was born in 1944, he at once suggested to the child's mother that a horoscope be made for the baby. In Malaysia too, high-ranking members of the administration take careful note of the times of their children's birth so that an accurate horoscope may be drawn up for them.

No one could regard these eminent believers in astrology as ignorant people who happen to have attained high office. They are men and women of intellectual sophistication, capable of meeting other world leaders on a basis of perfect equality. Interestingly enough, their belief in "the celestial science" is sometimes in contradiction to their political ideology. Thus the government of Sri Lanka, a coalition of Marxist groups that officially regard astrology as an outmoded superstition, have followed the advice of their country's Buddhist astrologers just as devoutly as their more conservative predecessors.

Many Western countries have also come under the influence of astrology at various times in their history, and astrology today claims many followers among the educated and the sophisticated in the West as in the East. Astrological forecasts appear in almost every popular magazine and newspaper in the Western world, and are eagerly read by millions. Whether they believe in astrology or not, most people would probably admit to sneaking at least an occasional glance at articles on astrology. The signs of the zodiac have become household words, and almost everyone knows whether he or she is a Piscean or Leo or Virgo.

Astrology—the subject that was once regarded as "the Queen of the Sciences"—has never been more popular. In both the United States and Europe every community of any size has dozens, sometimes hundreds, of professional astrologers, and thousands of amateur ones. Millions of horoscopes are cast every year in the United States alone. There are numerous magazines devoted exclusively to astrology, and other popular occult magazines are crammed with astrological advertisements. Although a good deal of criticism can be—and is—leveled at astrology, most people would probably like to believe that there could be something in it. But something in what exactly? What is the strange body of beliefs we call astrology?

Astrology is based on the belief that there is a relationship between the heavenly bodies and human beings, and that this relationship can be interpreted. More specifically, astrologers claim that the position of the Sun, Moon, and planets at the time and over the place of a person's birth has an important bearing on the kind of individual that person is and on the future course of his or her life. Astrologers believe that the planets are somehow bound up with the rhythms of human life, and that everyone and everything on Earth is affected by the cosmic conditions that prevailed at the time of a person's birth. Thus the planetary patterns at that moment are thought to indicate the pattern of a

Above: the coronation of Birendra Bir Bikram Shah Dev as king of Nepal and reincarnation of the Hindu god Vishnu in early 1975. The exact moment for his crowning by the high priest of the Court was determined by the Court astrologers, and the king had waited, uncrowned, for the most astrologically propitious day.

Right: a wax gypsy presides over a booth selling computer-produced horoscopes. Astrology has never been more broadly popular, and computer technology offers an obvious link-up, providing cheap individual horoscopes. But the need for mystery lives on—in spite of the convenience of science—and exotic, jewelry-laden Esmeraldas still have their part to play.

Belief in the influence of the planets and stars on the course of human life—the foundation of the system of astrology as we know it—is found worldwide, in societies and peoples so widely different that they share few other customs. Left: Maharaja Jai Singh II of India, a renowned mathematician, had this great observatory built in his new city of Jaipur to follow the track of the constellations of the zodiac across the sky during his reign in the 18th century.

newborn's personality and destiny throughout the rest of life.

Astrologers study these patterns by means of a horoscope or natal chart. This is a map of the zodiac—the band of sky within which the Sun, Moon, and planets appear to move—showing the exact position of all the planets at the time a person was born. Astrologers divide the zodiac into 12 zones represented by 12 different signs. The planets are thought to influence a person's life according to the signs they were in at the moment of birth, their distance from each other, and their exact location in the natal chart.

When astrologers began to write forecasts for magazines and newspapers they obviously could not publish a separate horoscope for each of their readers. They therefore devised a system

Above: three Babylonian carvings from boundary stones of the 10th century B.C., which have been interpreted as being signs of the zodiac. From left to right they are Sagittarius, Capricorn, Scorpio.

Below: an Aztec priest from a 16th-century Spanish history with pictures by Indian artists, shown observing a comet from a temple. The Aztecs were greatly concerned with all aspects of astrology and astronomy, and regarded comets in particular as evil portents. A year before Hernando Cortes and the conquering Spaniards arrived, a series of comets were sighted. Montezuma, the Aztec ruler, correctly interpreted them as a sign that his empire would fall.

of "Sun Signs" based simply on the date, rather than the precise time, of birth. So today when someone says "I'm a Leo," he means that he was born sometime between July 23 and August 23 when the Sun is located in the zone of the zodiac known as Leo. It was this use of Sun Signs that made astrology accessible to millions of ordinary people, and marked a new era in the long and sometimes star-crossed history of astrology.

The origins of astrology probably go back almost as far as humankind itself. Archeologists have recently unearthed a bone over 30,000 years old bearing marks that appear to refer to the phases of the Moon. Monuments like the great stone circle at Stonehenge in Britain are believed to have been sophisticated astronomical observatories, and to testify to prehistoric peoples' interest in the heavens. In the early cultures of Asia, Europe, and America, people constructed giant watchtowers and observatories so that their priests could search the night sky for the key to human destiny.

In was in the dry and cloudless climate of Mesopotamia, however, that astrology first emerged in something resembling its modern form. Five thousand years ago the priest-magicians of Babylon were already studying and naming the stars. By about 700 B.C. they had discovered the extent of the zodiac and had invented the 12 signs of the zodiac that we now know so well. They had attributed good and bad qualities to the planets and had begun to interpret *aspects*—the supposedly significant angles between one planet and another.

Astrology spread from Babylonia to Egypt and Greece. Some of the Egyptian pharaohs decorated their tombs with astrological symbols, but Egypt does not appear to have become enthusiastic about astrology until long after the golden age of the pharaohs and it was in Greece that astrology as we know it developed.

The Greeks identified the Sun, Moon, and planets with their own gods and goddesses. The planet Venus, for example, was identified with Aphrodite, goddess of love, and Jupiter with Zeus, the king of the gods. The Babylonians had judged the effect of a planet according to its appearance, believing that Jupiter had a favorable influence if it shone white and an unfavorable influence if it were red. The Greeks gave no importance to appearance. Instead they regarded planets as consistently favorable, a "benefic" or unfavorable, a "malefic." Zeus' planet Jupiter was a benefic while Mars, identified with Ares, the bloody

11

god of war, was a malefic. The Greeks also turned the planets into personalities, and combined the practical techniques of the Babylonian astrologers with the philosophies of their own great thinkers to add a moral significance to astrology.

The Greeks made personal horoscopes fashionable. They enabled a Babylonian astrologer to set up a school of astrology on the Greek island of Cos in 280 B.C., and from about 200 B.C. onward a number of widely circulated manuals were published on the subject. The most important of these was the *Tetrabiblos*, written in the second century A.D. by the Alexandrian Claudius Ptolemy, the greatest astronomer of ancient times.

Ptolemy's catalogs and atlases of the stars and planets were unmatched for accuracy until the 17th century, and his was probably the most influential book on astrology ever written. Ptolemy gathered together most of the astrological teachings of his own and preceding centuries in his book, which contained all the essentials that have gone to make up modern astrology, and included full details of how to calculate an individual horoscope.

By the time of Ptolemy, astrology had already captured the imagination of the Roman Empire. Rich man and poor, freeman and slave acknowledged its importance and accepted its doctrines. The great Augustus, first of the Roman Emperors, believed in it fully, perhaps partly because at the time of his birth the astrologer Nigidius had prophesied that he would become "master of the world." Augustus even stamped the sign of Capricorn—his birth sign—on some of the coinage he issued.

The main opponents of astrology in the ancient world were the early Christians. They saw astrology as being basically pagan and fatalistic, teaching that man has a fixed and unalterable future

Above: the Egyptian sky goddess Nut, surrounded by the signs of the zodiac, from a mummy case dating from the 2nd century A.D.

Right: a medieval miniature of the Greek Ptolemy, who lived in the 2nd century A.D. His great work *Tetrabiblos* gathered most of the astrological lore of the preceding centuries. He was concerned not only with movements of the stars as portents of the future, but for their own sake. His astronomy became the basis of all medieval study until his geocentric view was challenged by Copernicus in the 15th century.

instead of being able to change and redeem himself through baptism and the other sacraments of the Church. At first such opposition had little effect, for the early Church was a small and despised sect whose members were themselves the subject of harsh attack. In fact, many of the Christian denouncements of astrology were replies to those who condemned Christ as a magician, and accused his followers of crimes such as cannibalism and incest. However, with the growth of Christianity and its acceptance in the 4th century A.D. as the official religion of the Roman Empire, astrology gradually fell into disrepute, and its practitioners were regarded as little better than demon worshippers. By the time Rome fell to the barbarians in A.D. 410 there were few, if any, practicing astrologers left in the western half of the Empire, and within a few more decades the art had been largely forgotten.

In the Byzantine Empire of the East, however, astrological writings and techniques survived, and were passed on to the Arabs. Arab scholars made a serious study of astrology side by side with astronomy. They added to the work of their Greek predecessors, particularly in attaching importance to the motion and position of the Moon in the calculation of horoscopes.

It was through Latin translations of Arabic astrological texts that 12th-century European scholars rediscovered astrology. By the 16th century astrology had again become an acknowledged part of the cultural outlook of all men of learning. The great astronomers of the 16th and early 17th centuries, such as Johannes Kepler, were also practicing astrologers and regularly cast horoscopes as part of their work. Every king and prince had his Court Astrologer to advise him on matters of state. Astrology had by then become the true Queen of the Sciences.

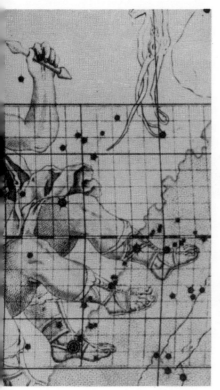

Left: the Greeks incorporated much of their mythology into their astrology by identifying gods with constellations. For example, the Gemini twins became Castor and Pollux, as shown in this 18th-century illustration in an atlas.

Below: this Roman coin minted in Spain depicts Capricorn, the zodiacal sign of Emperor Augustus.

St. Augustine and the Astrologers

The early Christians often came into conflict with the old beliefs of the ancient world, and astrology was one of the beliefs they most fiercely attacked. The stars, they said, could not be all-powerful because it was God that was omnipotent. Nor, they argued, could the stars determine a person's destiny, because free-will allows humans to decide their own future.

At first astrology held its own against all such attacks, especially since Christianity was itself in a struggle for survival. But at the end of the 4th century astrology was discredited by a group of militant Christians. The strongest and most influential of these was Saint Augustine—a man whose word was law in his day and whose influence on the whole development of Christianity was enormous.

In *City of God*, his last and longest work, Saint Augustine said of astrology: "Those who hold that stars manage our actions or our passions, good or ill, without God's appointment, are to be silenced and not to be heard . . . for what doth this opinion but flatly exclude all deity." He admitted that correct predictions occasionally occurred, but that they came from evil spirits and "not by any art of discerning of the Horoscope, for such is there none."

Still, Saint Augustine had once believed in the stars. What made him disbelieve and discredit the ancient art? He says in his *Confessions* it was because he had learned that a wealthy landowner and a lowly slave on that same rich man's estate had been born at the identical time. Their vastly different fates proved to him that the stars had nothing to do with destiny.

Above: after astrology in the West was gradually discarded, and the last traces buried by the barbarian influx, the Arabs kept the writings and techniques alive. In this illustration from a 17th-century Muslim design, an astrologer takes a reading of the position of a star. Near him is a model of the zodiac showing the 12 signs.

One of the best known of the 16th-century astrologers who acted as advisers to royalty was Dr. John Dee. This man was no mere stargazer, but a key figure in the intellectual life of his time. Born in 1527 of Welsh parents who had settled in London, Dee was a precocious child. He entered Cambridge University when he was only 15 years old, and throughout his time there he spent no less than 18 hours a day studying subjects that ranged from Greek to mechanics.

Dee continued his studies in the city of Louvain, now in Belgium, where he met and favorably impressed some of the greatest scientists of his age. All this time Dee was perfecting his knowledge of astrology and astronomy, and becoming adept at astrological calculation and interpretation.

Like many other scientists of his day, Dee was more attracted to the new Protestant interpretations of Christianity than to traditional Catholicism. He returned to England in the 1550s when the Catholic Queen Mary was persecuting the Protestants, and his religious views put his life at risk. At this time, Queen Mary's young half-sister, the future Queen Elizabeth I, who was known to have Protestant sympathies, was being kept a prisoner at Woodstock near Oxford. Queen Mary was under pressure from some of her Catholic advisers to get rid of her half-sister by whatever means possible, so Elizabeth was in fear of assassination throughout her imprisonment. She knew she was in danger of being executed on a trumped up charge of treason, or even of being killed by poison—a standby of 16th-century monarchs who wanted to dispose of dangerous rivals.

It is hardly surprising that Elizabeth was anxious to know what the future held in store for her, and she decided to consult an astrologer. It so happened that Blanche Parry, Elizabeth's confidential maid-in-waiting, was a cousin of John Dee, and on her recommendation Elizabeth turned to Dee for advice. Dee prepared an astrological forecast for Elizabeth, and also showed

Left: in this miniature from India, dating from about 1600, the casting of a birth chart for the newborn baby of the ruler is shown as a natural part of the celebrations. The astrologer's work goes on at the same time as the rejoicing.

Above: the astronomer Johannes
Kepler, born in 1571. Part of
his job as court mathematician to
Emperor Rudolf II in Prague was
to draw up horoscopes for the
emperor and other dignitaries.

her horoscopes he had calculated for Queen Mary and her husband Philip of Spain. Elizabeth's horoscope survives in the British Museum, and Dee's interpretation of it appears to have been accurate as well as optimistic. In letters secretly delivered to Elizabeth at Woodstock, Dee is thought to have told her that, although her situation was perilous, her life was in no danger. She was destined to rise to an outstanding position—perhaps to the throne itself—and would probably live to a ripe old age.

Dee's prophecies no doubt pleased and comforted Elizabeth, but the relationship between the two was soon discovered by Mary's secret agents. Dee was thrown into prison, accused not only of having unorthodox religious opinions, but also of showing a confidential document—Mary's horoscope—to Elizabeth and of practicing black magic. He was suspected of attempting to kill Queen Mary by sorcery so that Elizabeth could inherit the throne. Dee was eventually acquitted on all the charges for lack of evidence, but he spent some months languishing in jail. Even after his release he was forced to live in seclusion until Elizabeth came to the throne on Mary's death in 1558.

The new queen remembered Dee's services and regularly consulted him on astrological matters. Dee even decided the date of her coronation using a technique known as *electional astrology*—a method like that still used in many Eastern countries to determine the most favorable time for undertaking some new and important enterprise.

In spite of Queen Elizabeth's friendly regard for Dee she did not display favor too openly. Probably she felt that she could not afford to be publicly associated with a man who had twice been accused of sorcery and might be so again. However, she employed Dee as a secret agent in Europe, where he was believed to be one of her most trusted spies. Dee seems to have gathered some of his intelligence by conventional means—16th century equivalents of the techniques used today by the CIA and the Soviet Union's KGB—but most of the time he used astrology and other occult methods to predict the plans of England's enemies. He also made maps for the Queen and helped to draw up plans for naval defense.

Dee died in 1608 at the age of 81. Forty years after his death the science of the stars was still an influence in politics, and astrologers were playing an important role in the English Civil War—the struggle between Roundheads and Cavaliers to decide whether Parliament or King should rule the country. These astrologers were the psychological warfare experts of the time, producing predictions designed to keep up the morale of the partisans of each side. In London the astrologer William Lilly produced almanacs at more or less regular intervals. In them he prophesied the success of Parliament and the downfall of the Royalists. From Oxford, the headquarters of King Charles, Royalist astrologers published almanacs asserting exactly the opposite.

Not surprisingly these distortions of astrology for political ends tended to bring the art into disrepute. Thinking people concluded that if astrologers could produce diametrically opposite findings from identical sets of data—the positions of the Sun, Moon, and planets in the zodiac—their subject could

Left: Queen Elizabeth I dressed in her coronation robes. She was crowned on January 15, 1559, the date selected by John Dee (who had earlier cast her horoscope) as astrologically favorable for the beginning of a fortunate reign.

Below: Elizabeth I's birth chart. Born under Virgo, she had Saturn in Cancer in the Seventh House, the house of partners, which might be expected to indicate a delay in marriage. In fact, she died as she was crowned, a spinster queen.

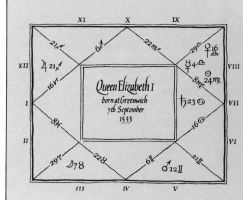

Queen Elizabeth I
born at Greenwich
7th September
1533

hardly be considered a science. The same conclusions were reached in Europe where astrology was used as a psychological weapon during the Thirty Years' War fought in central Europe from 1618 to 1648.

When their political opinions were not involved, however, certain 17th-century astrologers seem to have made some amazingly accurate predictions. Thus William Lilly, the astrologer who foresaw the Parliamentary victory, prophesied the 1665 outbreak of plague in London and the Great Fire of 1666 that followed it more than 10 years before these events took place. He expressed these predictions in the form of symbolic drawings, published as woodcuts in the early 1650s. Their meaning was so plain that Lilly was suspected of being involved

The Odd-looking Wizard of Wales

In the early part of the 17th century there lived a Welsh astrologer by the name of Evans. Most of what we know about him has come from his illustrious pupil William Lilly, who became well-known in England for his astrological predictions and writings.

Evans, it seems, was a curate —but not of the pious nature a man of the church should be. He had to leave his parish under pressure because of a scandalous offense.

As to his looks, he was somewhat formidable according to Lilly's description. He was "of a middle stature, broad forehead, down-looked, black curling stiff hair, splay footed." Of his character Lilly says: he was "much addicted to debauchery, and then very abusive and quarrelsome, seldom without a black eye, or some mischief or other."

Lilly decided to leave his master Evans when he discovered that the astrologer often told clients what they wanted to hear rather than what their horoscopes said.

For all of this, Evans must have had an attraction and following of some sort. There is an original drawing of him in the collection of the Right Honorable Lord Cardiff, from which the above engraving was made in 1776.

in a plot to start the Great Fire deliberately, and he was called before a parliamentary committee to explain how he had known about the fire in advance. Fortunately for the astrologer, he was able to convince the Members of Parliament who interrogated him that his predictions had been made on a purely astrological basis.

Successes such as those of Lilly kept the belief in astrology alive, but could not stop its decline. With few exceptions only the most old-fashioned scholars still regarded astrology as a science or discipline by the turn of the century. One exception was Sir Isaac Newton, the great philosopher and mathematician who defined the law of gravitation in the 1680s. He originally took up mathematics in order to practice astrology. Another was John Flamsteed, England's first Astronomer Royal. He took the subject so seriously that he used electional astrology to choose August 10, 1675 as the date for laying the foundation stone of the Royal Observatory at Greenwich.

As the 18th century wore on the practice of astrology almost completely died out in mainland Europe, and in England it was largely confined to the producers of yearly almanacs. These books were published shortly before the beginning of each new year. They included some astrological and astronomical information as well as lists of public holidays, farming hints, and other practical information. Their readers were mostly small farmers, and few of them probably had much faith in astrology to judge from the contents of some almanacs. The publisher of *Poor Robin's Almanac*, for instance, poked fun at astrology with jokes like, "Mars inclining to Venus ensureth that maids who walk out with soldiers on May morning will have big bellies by Christmas."

In the years 1780 to 1830, however, astrology enjoyed a small but significant revival in England. Perhaps because of an interest in the past that marked this period, old textbooks on the subject were reprinted. Some new texts were also written, and two astrological magazines were published. Once again it was possible to find professional as well as amateur astrologers.

These astrologers were a new breed—no longer men of learning, but occultists. These men and women combined their astrology with subjects such as alchemy—the supposed art of turning lead and other base metals into gold—fortune telling by the use of playing cards, and even the manufacture of talismans and other good luck charms.

The astrologers of this period also showed an excessive and gloomy preoccupation with the prediction of death. One of them, John Worsdale, published his analysis of 30 horoscopes in which he sought the dates of his clients' deaths, and he appears to have gained great satisfaction from telling these people of their impending doom. When a young girl named Mary Dickson approached him in August 1822 and asked him to predict the date of her marriage, Worsdale told her with apparent relish that "something of an awful nature would occur, before the Month of March, then next ensuing, which would destroy Life." Mary "laughed immoderately," but was sufficiently interested to ask Worsdale what would be the exact cause of her death. "I told her," reported the astute astrologer, "that it appeared

Right: William Lilly, the English astrologer. In the early 1650s he foresaw the Great Fire of London that devastated the city in 1666. He did not begin to study astrology until he was 30, when he was instructed by a Welshman "of indifferent abilities." He wrote that he started his studies out of curiosity to see if there was any truth in the whole business. He is shown here with a square birth chart held in his hand. (Ashmolean Museum, Oxford).

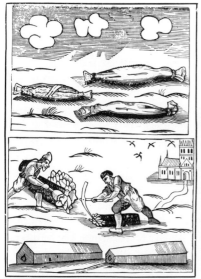

Above: Lilly also predicted the terrible outbreak of plague in London, which took place in 1665. This woodcut, which was published in 1651, represents such a vast number of dead that the supply of coffins is exceeded, and the bodies are buried in their shrouds—which in fact is exactly what happened during the terrible epidemic in which thousands died. Required by Parliament to explain how he knew what would happen, Lilly said he saw it in the stars.

to me that Drowning would be the cause of her Dissolution."

On the following January 7 Worsdale's prediction was fulfilled to the letter when Mary Dickson, who was traveling in a river boat, fell overboard and "when taken out life was found to be extinct."

The English astrological revival never completely receded. Throughout the 19th century astrology continued to attract people in Britain and the United States who were interested in the occult. After 1890 American and British astrology received a considerable boost from the occult revival launched by Madame H. P. Blavatsky and her Theosophical Society—founded in 1875 but not really important until the 1890s—and a host of lesser known occult societies that derived their astrological knowledge

Above: John Flamsteed, cleric and first Astronomer Royal of the observatory in Greenwich, England. It was established in 1675.

from India. These groups saw astrology as part of "the Ancient Wisdom"—traditional lore which, they believed, had been wrongly rejected by modern science—and they placed added emphasis on the occult aspects of the art.

Thus in the early 20th century Alan Leo, a British member of the Theosophical Society, wrote a whole series of influential astrological textbooks from the occult point of view. Leo was a highly successful astrologer who claimed that "every human being belongs to a Father Star in Heaven or a Star Angel as did Jesus Christ according to our scripture." (Even some of the early Christians who had clung to a belief in astrology saw the Star of Bethlehem as evidence of astrological truth, but most astrologers before Leo had denied that Christ was actually influenced by the Star of the Nativity.)

Leo's books were often written in obscure and confusing occult jargon, but he had skill in simplifying the techniques. He believed that "the problem of the inequalities of the human race can only be successfully solved by a knowledge of astrology," and much of his writing outlined astrological techniques in a clear way so that the ordinary reader could apply them for himself. With another astrologer, Leo also edited *The Astrologer's Magazine*—later renamed *Modern Astrologer*—whose first issue included the horoscopes of Jesus Christ, of Britain's Prince of Wales (later to become King Edward VII), and of the explorer Henry Morgan Stanley.

Leo's magazine was aimed at the general public, and his do-it-yourself books helped to transform 20th-century astrology. Until his writings simplified the subject, astrology required years of painstaking study and the mastery of comparatively advanced mathematics. With his books it became possible for anybody of reasonable intelligence to become a fairly competent astrologer after only a year or two of part-time study.

Left: a caricature of a fortune teller by Thomas Rowlandson in 1815 when astrology was in decline in Britain. The poem that accompanies the drawing tells us that the astrologer meets his death when his chair collapses—but he failed to predict it.

Below: the Royal Observatory, Greenwich, designed by Christopher Wren. Flamsteed selected the date for laying its foundation stone by using electional astrology. It was duly laid August 10, 1675.

The result was explosive. As Leo's books were reprinted in the United States and published in German translation, and as others imitated his approach, a host of new astrologers—some amateur and some professional—joined the ranks of the old guard. By 1930 most Americans, Britons, and Germans who were at all interested in the world of the occult knew at least one person capable of casting and interpreting a horoscope.

Probably the most famous of the astrologers who learned their art from Leo's books was Evangeline Adams. Born in 1865, she was a descendant of John Quincy Adams, sixth president of the United States, and she seems to have inherited his determination and sense of purpose. Believing in her own reading of her stars, she made a move to New York City from her hometown of Boston in 1899. She created an immediate sensation. On her first night in the hotel she had booked into, she read the horoscope of the proprietor and warned him of a dreadful disaster. The next day the hotel burned down—and the proprietor's report of her warning to the newspapers put her name in the headlines. Evangeline Adams so gained the kind of publicity that more than offset the loss of much of her belongings in the fire. She set up a business as a reader of horoscopes, and was soon on the way to becoming America's most popular astrologer.

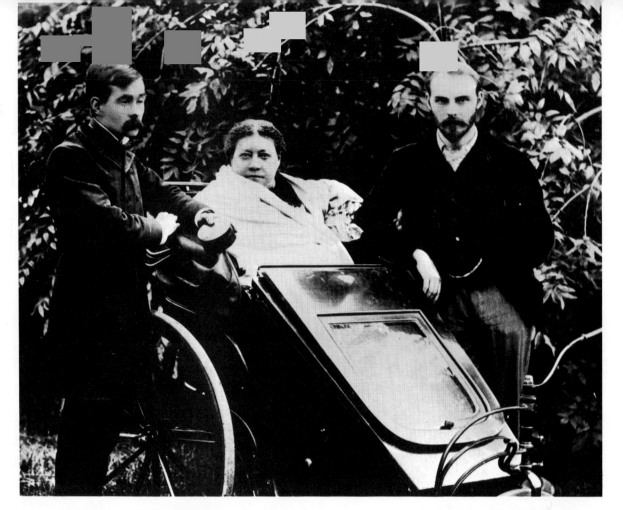

Above: Madame Blavatsky, founder of the Theosophical Society, with two of her colleagues in 1875. Her society appears to have mainly encountered astrology through its enthusiasm with the wisdom of India, in which astrology played a long-standing and very important role.

Left: Alan Leo, one of the first modern popularizers of astrology, shown in his own horoscope. After Leo's death in 1917, people wrote to his widow that he was still teaching astrology and theosophy to them "on the astral plane." On a more earthly level, his books had a tremendous impact, educating a new generation of astrologers.

In spite of—or perhaps because of—her success, Evangeline Adams was arrested for fortune telling in 1914. Although she could have elected to pay a fine and go free, she decided to stand trial and argue her own defense. Armed with a pile of reference books, she told the court precisely how she made her analyses and predictions. To prove her point, she offered to make a reading from the birth date of someone she had never met, without even knowing who that person was. The person chosen was the judge's son, and this judge was so impressed with her reading that he concluded, "The defendant raises astrology to the dignity of an exact science." Evangeline Adams was acquitted, and in New York at least astrology was no longer regarded as fortune telling.

Evangeline Adams' triumph had struck an important blow for the respectability of astrology. She proceeded to open a studio in Carnegie Hall in New York City, where she was consulted by politicians, Hollywood stars, royalty, and Wall Street tycoons. Her clients included the Duke of Windsor, Mary Pickford, Caruso, and the financier J. P. Morgan for whom she provided regular forecasts concerning politics and the stock market. There is evidence that many of her clients took her advice seriously, using it as the basis for major decisions regarding their careers, investments, and political activities. Certainly they paid her substantial fees, and by the 1920s she was a wealthy woman.

In 1930 Evangeline Adams began a series of regular radio broadcasts on astrology, and within a year she was receiving 4000 requests a day from listeners who wanted her to cast their horoscope. Her book *Astrology: Your Place Among the Stars* became a best seller, and a number of present-day astrologers first became acquainted with the subject through it. Nevertheless, Evangeline Adams did not escape attacks on her character. It was said that she was not the true author of most of her book. Aleister Crowley, the notorious British magician and a keen amateur astrologer, claimed that he had written the book for Evangeline Adams in return for a fee—a fee that Crowley maintained he had never received. Many of the horoscopes analyzed in the book were for people whom Crowley particularly admired, such as the 19th-century explorer Sir Richard Burton.

Such attacks did nothing to cloud Evangeline Adams' reputation, however. Throughout 1931 her radio show continued to bring her masses of mail from fans who regarded her as a kindly adviser and friend. In that year, Evangeline Adams prophesied that the United States would be at war in 1942, and the following year she is said to have forecast her own death. She explained that she would be unable to undertake a lecture tour for late 1932, and in November of that year she died.

Such was Evangeline Adams' popularity that the public flocked to the Carnegie Hall studio where her body lay in state. Crowds of fans attended her funeral, and there were thousands of telegrams of condolence. No one before Evangeline Adams had done so much to bring astrology to the attention of the general public. By the time of her death, she had become the most popular and successful astrologer of our century—and possibly of all time.

By comparison, the career of another well-known woman

Above: Evangeline Adams, who helped make astrology respectable as well as popular. A woman of courage and determination, she has been quoted as saying, "I have Mars conjunct my natal Sun in the 12th house. I will always triumph over my enemies!" In fact she was immensely successful, and from about 1914 to 1932 her clients included the great and the wealthy.

astrologer was played out in a more muted key. Elsbeth Ebertin was an honest, competent, and totally unaffected German astrologer, who was born in 1880 and commenced her professional life as a *graphologist*—an interpreter of character from the study of a person's handwriting.

In 1910 Elsbeth Ebertin met a woman who also claimed to be a graphologist, and who was able to give accurate delineations of character. Yet in talking to her, Elsbeth Ebertin discovered that this woman did not even know the basic principles of graphology. It turned out that she was really an astrologer, but preferred not to admit this to her clients because few of them had even heard of astrology.

Impressed by this woman's ability, Elsbeth Ebertin decided to become a professional astrologer herself. She started to study textbooks issued by a small publishing house called the Astrological Library. These included German translations of Alan Leo's writings and books by Karl Brandler-Pracht, an occultist who was busily engaged in reviving German astrology. By 1918 Elsbeth Ebertin had become a competent astrological practitioner, publicist, and writer. She had a sizeable private clientele, gave lectures on astrology, and published at regular intervals an almanac called *A Glimpse Into the Future*, containing predictions of the future of Germany and the world.

The first issue of *A Glimpse Into the Future* was published in 1917, and the almanac then and later was often impressively accurate in its forecasts. One of Elsbeth Ebertin's most famous predictions was contained in the July 1923 edition. It read: "A man of action born on April 20, 1889, with Sun in the 29th degree of Aries at the time of his birth, can expose himself to personal danger by excessively rash action and could very likely trigger off an uncontrollable crisis. His constellations show that this man is to be taken very seriously indeed. He is destined to play a 'Führer-role' in future battles . . . The man I have in mind, with this strong Aries influence, is destined to sacrifice himself for the German nation, and also to face up to all circumstances with audacity and courage, even when it is a matter of *life and death*, and to give an impulse, which will burst forth quite suddenly . . . But I will not anticipate destiny. Time will show . . ."

In fact Elsbeth Ebertin's forecast anticipated destiny rather well. The "man of action born on April 20, 1889" was none other than Adolf Hitler. In November 1923, four months after Elsbeth Ebertin's prediction, he launched an "excessively rash action"—the unsuccessful Munich *Putsch*. This was the attempt by Hitler, then a relatively obscure political adventurer, to overthrow the legally constituted German government by force. It resulted in the killing of a number of his followers—members of the infant Nazi party. Hitler himself dislocated his shoulder during the fighting and served a term of imprisonment for treason.

As for the rest of Elsbeth Ebertin's prediction, that too was fulfilled. Hitler did indeed play a "'Führer-role' in future battles." In spite of his destructive nature it could be said that he "faced up to all circumstances with audacity and courage," and at the end of his life, in the burning ruins of Berlin, he committed suicide—or, as he himself expressed it to his intimates in the very words of the

Right: the German astrologer Elsbeth Ebertin. She was a gifted journalist with the ability to write about astrology in a simple and interesting fashion. When sent Hitler's birth date in 1923 from one of his many enthusiastic women supporters in Munich, she published a prediction that "a man of action" born that day was "destined to play a 'Führer-role' in future battles." Although her prediction was uncannily accurate, she was wrong about his Sun being in Aries—because her correspondent had not sent Hitler's birth hour. He was born at 6.30 p.m., by which time the Sun had passed into Taurus.

Right: Adolf Hitler surrounded by some of his many women admirers. In this case they are Austrian girls he met during the May Day celebrations in Berlin in 1939.

famous astrologer, "sacrificed himself for the German people."

Elsbeth Ebertin continued publishing her almanac until 1937, when she was apparently forced to close it down as a result of pressure from the Gestapo. Possibly some of her past prophecies came too close to the truth for comfort, and the outspoken nature of her predictions may have made the Nazis fear that publications like hers could exert a political influence not to their taste.

Nevertheless, Elsbeth Ebertin kept up her private practice until her death in an air raid in November 1944. According to her son Reinhold, a distinguished German astrologer of the present day, his mother foresaw the bomb that killed her, but felt she should not move to possible safety out of regard for her neighbors. They took comfort from her continued presence among them, saying "As long as Frau Ebertin is here nothing very much can happen to us."

Since the end of World War II astrology has had a boom. All over the world institutes now exist for the serious study of astrology, and in 1960 Harvard University accepted a thesis on astrology for the B.A. degree. The American Federation of Astrologers and the British Faculty of Astrological Studies have thousands of members who pass examinations for a diploma in their subject, and subscribe to a code of ethics. Interest in

astrology has never been greater. But can we really believe in horoscopes today?

The successful career of Carroll Righter might indicate that many people still do. At the age of 75 years, Righter is the dean of American astrologers—not just in age, but also in status. He might be said to have taken the mantle from Evangeline Adams, whom he met when he was only 14 years old. As a friend of the family she cast his horoscope and found him likely to be a skillful interpreter of the stars. She urged him to become an astrologer. Some 25 years went by before he finally followed her advice, but when he did, he fast became a leader in the field. Based in Hollywood, he has counted among his clients such past and present stellar names as Tyrone Power, Susan Hayward, Marlene Dietrich, and Ronald Colman. It is thought that he might be a millionaire with earnings from numerous newspaper and magazine columns, day-by-day astrological forecasts, and books on how astrology can help in business and finance, and in marriage and family relationships.

Before he became a professional astrologer in 1939, Righter had been in law practice and had also worked on civic projects. During the Depression he began to use astrology to help the unemployed. He found that he could help direct people to jobs by showing them what their horoscopes said they were best suited for. This made many of them look for work that they might never have considered otherwise.

Another astrologer whose career seems to show that there is a place for astrology in modern life is Katina Theodossiou. This well-known British practitioner is one of the world's foremost business astrologers. She is consultant to more than 50 companies in the United States and Europe, giving advice on such matters as mergers, takeovers, staffing, and investment. Many a company has even been born at the time and on the date that she has suggested by the guidance of the stars.

Katina Theodossiou has also helped bring astrology into the computer age. In one assignment for a New York firm, she programmed a computer in order to produce computerized horoscopes for sale. It was a notable success. She worked on the project for 15 months during which time she fed 40,000 separate items of astrological information into the machine.

Astrologers themselves are divided on the subject of computer horoscopes, but few if any would call Katina Theodossiou to account for insincerity or incompetence.

Astrology has never lacked its critics, however, and there are many people today who would not hesitate to dismiss the subject as a ridiculous and outmoded set of doctrines appealing only to the naive and superstitious. Serious astrologers are the first to admit that their art contains a number of inconsistencies and vague assumptions that are difficult to verify. Still they are convinced that astrology is based on truth, and that it can play a valuable role in helping human beings understand more about themselves and their place in the Universe. Today some orthodox scientists are coming to share their point of view. The very people who have long been most skeptical of astrology are now providing evidence to suggest that the ancient art of astrology may be founded on fact.

Above: the current enthusiasm for astrology, like other fads, finds avid fans in Hollywood. There an interior decorator designs rooms for homes and offices that harmonize with the astrological character readings of the occupants. Right: today the signs of the zodiac are familiar to people in all walks of life. One executive in the entertainment world even has a zodiac in his Hollywood pool.

Above: Katina Theodossious, British astrologer. She is not herself clairvoyant, and insists that "astrology is pure science, the oldest science in the world." Her no-nonsense approach has clearly helped her become established as a business astrologer, giving advice to many commercial clients.

2

Astrology is For Real

In March 1951 John H. Nelson, an American electronic and radio engineer, published a sensational article. There was nothing sensational about the journal in which the article appeared, however. That was the straight-forward *RCA Review*, a technical journal published by the Radio Corporation of America and devoted to all aspects of radio, television, and electronics. Nelson's article was an equally serious account of his research into factors affecting radio reception. But his report was to shatter orthodox views about humans and the Universe, for his findings appeared to confirm the basic belief of astrology—that the planets can and do

Our century is a skeptical one, and for astrology to be taken seriously—and not dismissed as superstitious nonsense that has outlived its time—it now has to prove itself in the rigorous court of science. Much to many of the scientists' astonishment, in some ways astrology seems to have met the test, with statistical evidence that traditional claims of the influence of planetary positions are being triumphantly vindicated.

Right: a 15th-century illustration of Saturn with the signs of the zodiac and the professions which that planet is supposed to govern. This link between the planetary position at the time of birth and the profession that a person follows is an aspect of astrology which has been supported by statistics.

"Was it the result of some unknown cosmic influence?"

Below: John H. Nelson, an electronic and radio engineer who did research on the relationship between the position of the planets and the quality of radio reception. He found that certain planetary positions can make reception poor.

influence our lives. The story behind Nelson's article began when RCA scientists noticed an apparent connection between the difficulty or ease of shortwave radio communication and the varying positions of the Earth's planetary neighbors. Was this link pure coincidence, RCA wanted to know, or was it the result of some hitherto unknown cosmic influence?

The first step in answering this question was to set up a basic statistical investigation of the phenomenon. RCA asked several astronomers to undertake this task, but all refused. In their opinion the idea that planetary positions could affect radio waves was so ridiculous that it was not worth investigating. However, RCA was unwilling to abandon the inquiry, and assigned Nelson, an experienced radio engineer, to investigate.

As Nelson checked records of radio disturbance dating back to the 1920s he made a series of exciting discoveries. He found that magnetic storms—the cause of radio disturbance—occur when two or more planets, viewed from the Earth, are very close together at right angles to one another or 180° apart. The position of the planets did appear to influence radio reception, and in a way that came as no surprise to the astrologers. These particular relationships—the aspects—between the planets have been important in astrology since ancient times, and none of them is regarded as favorable. The *conjunction*—when the planets are very close together on the same side of the Sun—is considered neutral, being good or bad according to certain factors modifying it. When the planets are in *square*—at right angles to one another—it is seen as disharmonious, difficult, and even evil. The same applies when planets are in *opposition*—180° apart on opposite sides of the Sun.

Nelson's subsequent discoveries also tied in with traditional astrological beliefs. He discovered that magnetic disturbances were notably absent, and that shortwave reception was therefore good, when two or more planets were 60° or 120° apart. These are precisely the aspects that astrology regards as harmonious, easy, and good. Further, Nelson found that aspects of 150° and 135° also had an effect on radio reception—a discovery of particular interest since these aspects were not used by astrologers of the ancient world, but are used by many present-day ones.

The test of a scientific theory is whether it enables the accurate prediction of future events. While Nelson had discovered a number of fascinating correlations between planetary positions and radio reception, they just might have been the result of chance. The real question was whether Nelson could use his findings to predict future magnetic disturbances.

He tried—and his predictions were 80 percent accurate. Later, by refining his methods to include details of all the planets, he

Right: this diagram shows the kind of planetary grouping that would coincide with magnetic storms and poor radio reception on Earth, according to a theory developed by Nelson for predicting periods of radio disturbance. In this configuration foretelling trouble in the way of a magnetic storm (X), Mercury (A) is in *square* or 90° to Venus (B) and Mars (C); Saturn (D) is in *opposition* or 180° to Earth; and Jupiter (E) is in *square* to both Earth and Saturn.

increased his success rate to an amazing 93 percent. Nelson had provided the first piece of scientific evidence to show that life on Earth could be influenced by the planets, and the claims of the astrologers—for long regarded as totally irrational—were seen to have some justification.

Nelson's discovery was not an isolated one. Other work carried out by scientists in recent years had also tended to back up astrology's basic beliefs about the influence of the Sun, Moon, and planets on earthly events and on people themselves.

For example, the late Dr. Rudolf Tomaschek, an academic physicist and chairman of the World Geophysical Council, made a statistical analysis of 134 large earthquakes. He found that planetary positions in relationship to the place and time these earthquakes occurred were highly significant. The "earthquake aspects" almost always included one or more of the planets Jupiter, Uranus, and Neptune, and the stronger the earthquake the more likely these planets were to be involved—usually in traditionally sinister aspects such as the square.

Dr. Tomaschek believed in astrology so that, in spite of his academic qualifications, some people were skeptical of his findings. The same criticism could not be leveled at the work of Dr. A. K. Podshibyakin, a Soviet physician who discovered a remarkable connection between physical events on the Sun and the incidence of road accidents in the Soviet Union.

Dr. Podshibyakin's findings, published in 1967, were based on statistics compiled over a number of years at Tomsk Medical College. These studies showed that the day after a solar flare—a magnetic storm on the surface of the Sun—there was a marked increase in road accidents, sometimes to as much as four times the daily average. Dr. Podshibyakin pointed out that this link between solar flares and road accidents was not confined to the Soviet Union, but had also been observed by researchers in West Germany. He gave a possible explanation of the phenomenon, based on the known fact that a solar flare produces a tremendous amount of ultraviolet radiation, which causes changes in the Earth's atmosphere. Dr. Podshibyakin suggested that this radiation affects the human body, slowing it down.

No such explanation can be provided for even stranger influences produced by the Sun and Moon on earthly life—influences that have astonished and puzzled the scientists who have observed them. One such scientist is Dr. Frank A. Brown, Professor of Biology at Northwestern University.

For the last 25 years Brown and his team have been conducting research into "biological clocks"—the natural rhythms shown by all life on Earth. These clocks manifest themselves in many ways, from the regular sleeping and waking patterns of human beings to the small movements made by certain plants during the night. There have been many efforts to explain the nature of these life rhythms, varying from the idea that they are the response of living beings to air ionization, to the suggestion that each separate organism possesses its own internal timing mechanism—a biological clock in the strict meaning of the term.

None of these explanations satisfied Dr. Brown. He found it impossible, for example, to trace any mechanism by which air ionization could trigger off the purposeful and meaningful acti-

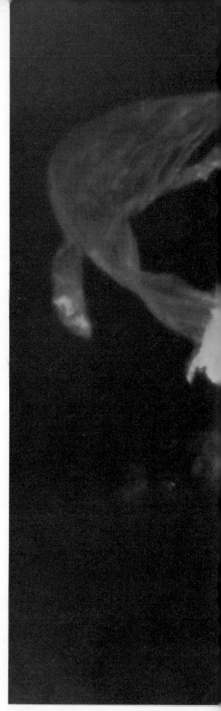

vities of life rhythms. Equally, he was unable to find any physical
organ in living beings that could serve as a mechanical clock.

Over a 10-year period Brown and his associates ran experiments on a variety of phenomena. These included the movement
of bean plants in the night, the amount of running performed by
caged rats during successive days, the sleep pattern of flies, the
opening and closing of oyster shells, and changes in the color of
fiddler crabs.

What emerged was astonishing. All these phenomena followed
rhythmical cycles, and those cycles were triggered not by some
internal clock, but by cosmic influences—notably those connected with the Sun and the Moon. Thus, for example, rats living
under controlled conditions in darkened cages were found to be

Above: Dr. Frank A. Brown Jr. of Northwestern University. His research into biological clocks have produced fascinating evidence of a direct link between the behavior of living things and the Sun and the Moon—just what the astrologers have always asserted.

twice as active when the Moon was above the horizon as when it was below it. They seemed to know instinctively when the Moon was up and responded to it, although they had no way of seeing it.

Equally surprising was the behavior of oysters. When they are in their natural habitat, oysters open and close their shells according to the rhythm of the tides. At high tide they open their shells to feed, and at low tide they close them as a protection against drying out. While the tides are, of course, produced by the gravitational pull of the Moon and Sun, it had always been assumed that the movement of the tides alone caused the opening and closing of the oysters' shells. No one had ever been bold enough to suggest that the oysters were responding directly to the Moon and Sun. Yet Brown discovered that they were apparently doing just that.

What Dr. Brown had done was to remove some oysters from the Atlantic seaboard of the United States, and place them in darkened containers so that no sunlight or moonlight could reach them. He had then taken them to his laboratory in Evanston, Illinois, a thousand miles from the sea. Within a fortnight the oysters had lost the pattern of opening and closing that they had displayed in their old home in the Atlantic, and were following the rhythm of what the tides would have been in Evanston had that town been on the sea. In other words, the oysters were not directly influenced by the tides, but by some other signals apparently related to the Moon and Sun.

What about people? Do the Sun, Moon, and planets really affect us, as astrologers claim? A study published in 1960 by another American scientist, Dr. Leonard Ravitz of Duke University, has shown a direct link between the behavior of human beings and the Moon. His findings coincide with the age-old belief that there is a connection between the Moon and madness.

Over a long period Ravitz plotted the variations in the small electric charges that are continually given off by the human body. He worked with both the mentally ill and a control group of healthy people. He found that the body's electrical potential underwent regular changes in all the people tested, and that these changes coincided with the phases of the Moon. The most marked changes occurred when the Moon was full, and the more disturbed the patient, the greater was the extent of the change.

Dr. Ravitz was therefore able to predict emotional changes in his mental patients, and to confirm that the full Moon does tend to provoke crises in people whose mental balance is already disturbed. "Whatever else we may be we are all electric machines," says Ravitz. "Thus energy reserves may be mobilized by periodic universal factors, such as the forces behind the Moon, which tend to aggravate maladjustments and conflicts already present."

The rhythms of the Moon may also have some effect on the patterns of human birth. Not enough research has been done on this subject to come to any definite conclusions, but it is interesting to note that in 1938 a Japanese scientist made a study of the cosmic factors in 33,000 live births. He found that high numbers of births occurred at the full and new Moons and low numbers one or two days before the Moon's first and last quarters. According to a report published in 1967 an American gynecologist has confirmed these findings from a study of no less than

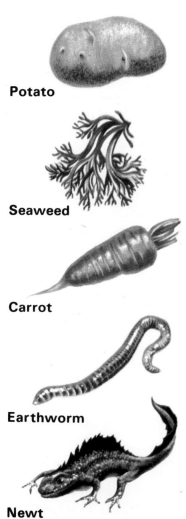

Potato

Seaweed

Carrot

Earthworm

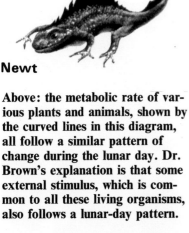

Newt

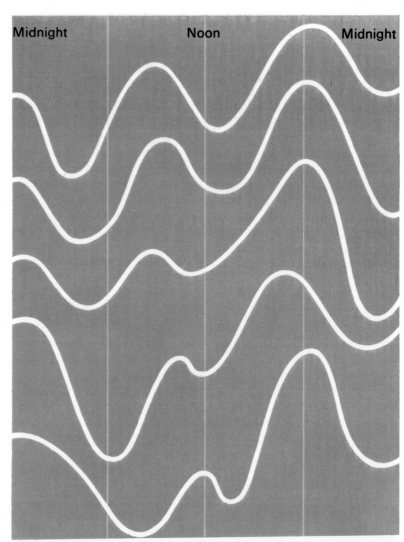

Midnight   Noon   Midnight

Above: the metabolic rate of various plants and animals, shown by the curved lines in this diagram, all follow a similar pattern of change during the lunar day. Dr. Brown's explanation is that some external stimulus, which is common to all these living organisms, also follows a lunar-day pattern.

Right: normally fiddler crabs change from a dark color during the day to a light color at night. If kept in constant darkness they will continue to change color in the way normal to them. But if they are subjected to a new 24-hour cycle of light and dark, they reset their biological clock and change color according to the new time. Then if once again returned to constant darkness, the crabs go by the new time cycle.

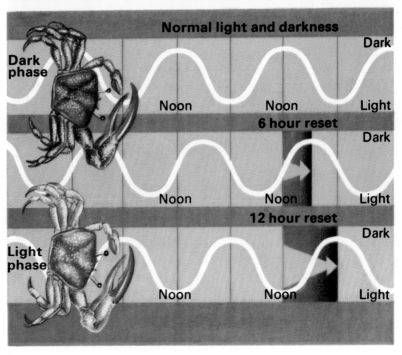

Normal light and darkness

Dark

Dark phase

Noon   Noon   Light

6 hour reset

Dark

Noon   Noon   Light

12 hour reset

Dark

Light phase

Noon   Noon   Light

half a million births. This evidence at least supports the theory.

The date of a person's birth depends of course on the time of conception, and this in turn depends on the time of ovulation—the release of an egg from the ovary. Psychiatrist Eugen Jonas of Czechoslovakia has discovered a clear connection between the time of ovulation and the Moon. His studies have shown that a woman tends to ovulate during the particular phase of the Moon that prevailed when she was born. Jonas has even used his findings to provide women in Eastern Europe with a new and entirely natural method of contraception. His charts, drawn up to show the days on which a woman can conceive, have proved 98 percent effective—as efficient as the contraceptive pill.

It has long been believed that a woman's menstrual cycle, with its average of 28 days or the length of time between two full Moons, is in some way connected with the rhythms of the Moon, and there is some scientific evidence to support this view. At the beginning of this century, Swiss chemist Dr. Svante Arrhenius made a study of 11,000 women. He found that the onset of menstruation reached a peak at the new Moon. In the 1960s two German researchers, who had kept records of the onset of menstruation in 10,000 women over a period of 14 years, came to a similar conclusion.

There is certainly evidence of a connection between bleeding in general and the phases of the Moon. The American physician Dr. Edson Andrews found, for example, that in 1000 cases of unusually heavy bleeding following tonsillectomies, 82 percent of the bleeding crises occurred between the Moon's first and third quarters. "These data have been so conclusive," said Dr. Andrews, ". . . that I threaten to become a witch doctor and operate on dark nights only."

These are only a fraction of the discoveries scientists have made concerning the influence of cosmic events on life on Earth. Many other experiments also make it clear that the Sun, Moon, and planets seem to exert a profound effect on us and our environment, and that the basic belief of the astrologers is in no way unscientific. Has this led any scientists to a belief in astrology?

Some—but not very many. Nevertheless, the scientists who have come to accept the fundamental claims of astrology have often been outstanding in their fields. The late Carl G. Jung, whom many consider to have been the greatest psychologist of the 20th century, was outspoken in his admiration for this traditional art. He claimed that astrology would eventually have to be recognized as a science. "The cultural philistines," he said, "believed until recently that astrology had been disposed of long since and today could safely be laughed at, but today, arising out of the social deeps, it knocks at the doors of the universities from which it was banished some 300 years ago."

Jung believed so profoundly in astrology that in later life he insisted on having a horoscope for each of his patients. He maintained that the horoscope provided an excellent guide to character and psychological disposition. He also carried out some elementary observations to test the ancient astrological belief that there are significant interactions between the planetary positions in the horoscopes of married couples.

Above: Dr. Eugen Jonas. His research convinced him he had discovered a clear connection between the time of ovulation and the Moon, which provided him with a method of natural contraception. Some claim a 98 percent success rate. Below: Dr. C. G. Jung, the world-famous psychologist. He carried out a study of the horoscopes of married couples to see if aspects that are traditionally considered to favor marriage did in fact appear. He judged the results inconclusive.

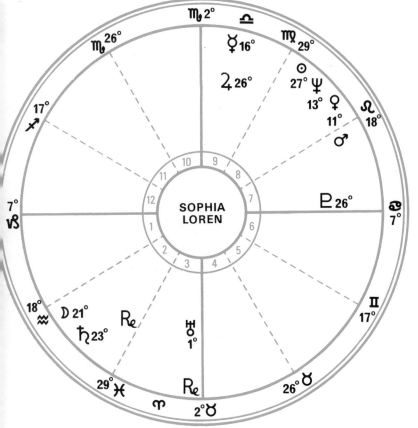

Elizabeth Taylor

Love and marriage are subjects of great interest both to readers and writers of popular astrology. These horoscopes of two famous and beautiful women come from a best-selling astrological magazine. Elizabeth Taylor's birth chart shows her Sun Sign is Pisces, with Libra ascending, a romantic and glamourous blend. But Venus conjoins Uranus, which indicates sexual excitement. Both are in the Seventh House, the house of marriage, a configuration portending sudden brutal terminations. Of her six marriages, four have ended in divorce and one in sudden death (Mike Todd in an air crash). The Moon on the Third House cusp predicts her femininity, but its position in Scorpio produces an aggressive, hard-hitting nature. In general, Pisceans delight in illusions, fantasies, the stuff of romance. But they can also be sloppy, forgetful, and unpunctual.

Sophia Loren

The same astrologer finds a very different birth chart for this Italian star. Her Sun Sign is Virgo with Capricorn rising—both earthy signs, frequently pointing to a peasant shrewdness. Saturn rules her personally and colors her outlook that one is safest with older people, looks don't matter, money means security. Coming out of a childhood of wartime poverty, Sophia Loren is now very rich, which is predictable from Saturn's position in the Second House of money. An awkward placing of the planets Jupiter, Uranus, and Pluto points to difficulties in marriage, and certainly the star and Carlo Ponti have had trouble legalizing their union. But the Sun (which represents a woman's husband) is in an excellent aspect with Pluto, so the marriage should be a happy one—and seems to be outside the legal complications.

37

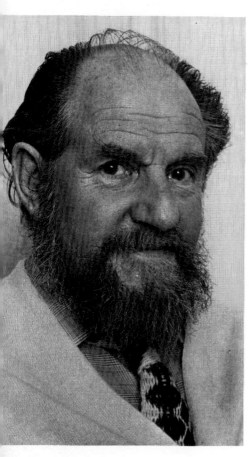

Above: John Addey, British philosopher, statistician, and astrologer. By means of statistics he studied the relationship between long life and the position of the planets at the time of birth. He found a significant connection.

Jung's experimental work was by no means complete, but he did find significant Sun-Moon interrelationships in the horoscopes of the 483 married couples he studied. In pairing off the horoscopes of husband and wife Jung found, for example, that the woman's Moon was frequently in conjunction with the man's Sun—the aspect that astrologers claim most favors marriage.

In recent years Jung's approach to astrological research has found favor with a number of investigators, among them the British philosopher John M. Addey, a dedicated astrologer who is also a competent statistician. Surprisingly enough, Addey's work sprang originally from a feeling that there was a good deal wrong with astrology in its traditional form. "So far as the practical rules . . . are concerned there are a host of uncertainties," he said, ". . . intractable problems which can only be solved by careful, persistent work; . . . our records are scattered and contain many errors . . . The chief obstacle is the opposition of the scientific fraternity, and to silence or check their criticism would seem to be the first step in presenting our case to a wider public . . ."

Addey's first attempt to "silence or check" continuing scientific objections to astrology involved 970 people over 90 years of age whose names appeared in the British *Who's Who*—a biographical directory of the eminent in all walks of life. A horoscope was prepared for each of these long-lived people, and all the horoscopes were compared to see if they had any factors in common.

Addey first checked to see if there was any truth in the ancient astrological tradition that people born under certain Sun Signs are more likely to be long lived than others. No such connection was found. The traditionally long-lived Capricornians, for instance, were no better represented among the 90-year-olds than the traditionally short-lived Pisceans. Addey did, however, discover one remarkable link in the horoscopes of his long-lived subjects. This concerned aspects—the relationships between two or more planets standing at significant angles to one another. Astrologers have always divided aspects into two types: *applying*—when a fast-moving planet is moving *into* a significant angle with a slow-moving planet; and *separating*—when a fast-moving planet is moving *away* from such a position. Addey found that the horoscopes of his 90-year-olds showed a preponderance of separating aspects.

This is precisely what one would expect if there is any truth in astrology, for astrologers have always held that separating aspects indicate the conservation of physical and mental energy, relaxation, and passivity—just the characteristics likely to be found in people who manage to live into their nineties.

Was this result merely a fluke? Addey decided to investigate another group of people with characteristics as opposite those of the 90-year-olds as possible—people who would be likely to expend their energies, be tense, nervous, and active. If the preponderance of separating aspects in the horoscopes of the 90-year-olds was more than a coincidence, then the opposite group should show an equivalent preponderance of applying aspects.

The group that Addey selected for his investigation was one

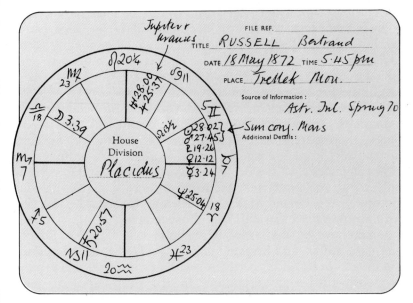

Left: Bertrand Russell's birth chart, as worked out by Addey. The Sun position, just separating from conjunction with Mars and a sextile with Jupiter, is typical of the planetary aspects found in charts of the 970 notable people of 90 years of age or over whom Addey took as his sample group. Below: Bertrand Russell, the British philosopher who became world-renowned for his vigorous defense of individual liberty. He was an avowed pacifist, and his views on sexual morality made him a controversial figure. He was not exactly the relaxed and passive individual that might be indicated by his horoscope. However, he did live to the ripe old age of 98.

to which he himself belonged—people who had been physically handicapped to some extent following an attack of polio. He chose this group because it is generally accepted by physicians that most polio victims who suffer long-term damage from the disease are of a particular physical and mental type. They tend to be athletically active rather than sedentary, alert rather than sluggish and plodding, and outgoing rather than introspective. When the horoscopes of the polio group were analyzed they completely fulfilled Addey's expectations. Their case was exactly the opposite of the long-lived sample—it showed a significant preponderance of applying aspects.

Addey was, of course, predisposed to a belief in astrology. Other statistical investigations have been carried out by researchers with a far more skeptical approach to the subject. The most outstanding work of this kind has been produced by the French scientist and statistician Michel Gauquelin, who began his research in 1950 with the object of *disproving* astrology.

Gauquelin's first step was to examine the sets of supposed statistical evidence in favor of astrology which had been produced earlier in the century by the astrological writers Paul Choisnard, Karl Krafft, and Leon Lasson. Using advanced statistical techniques Gauquelin had no difficulty in showing that all the evidence produced by Choisnard and Krafft rested on too small test groups or faulty mathematical methods. There remained the work of Lasson, who had investigated planetary positions in relation to people's professions, and had produced some surprising results. Lasson had found that, in an exceptionally high number of cases, Mars figures prominently in the horoscopes of medical men, Venus in the horoscopes of artists, and Mercury in those of actors and writers.

Gauquelin concluded that Lasson's test groups had probably been too small and decided to run an analysis of his own, using the horoscopes of 576 medical academics. To his amazement, he found that an unusually high percentage of these men had been born when Mars or Saturn was either coming over the horizon or passing its highest point in the sky. Gauquelin then checked

Above: a 16th-century woodcut of Mars as the patron of certain occupations, mainly military. These traditional ideas were long dismissed as purely superstitious until the French scientist Michel Gauquelin produced statistical results suggesting that a person's choice of profession had a definite relationship to the positions of planets at his or her birth.

his findings with a new test group of 508 eminent physicians. Mars and Saturn were prominent in exactly the same way. Taking the two test groups together, the odds against these planetary positions being due to chance were ten million to one.

Gauquelin's results received widespread and favorable coverage in the French press. Their reception by Gauquelin's fellow statisticians and scientists was less favorable. Some claimed that Gauquelin's test groups must have been insufficient; others said that he had merely discovered a national peculiarity, since all his subjects were French. "Your conclusions are nothing but pulp romances . . ." the Belgian scientist Marcel Boll told Gauquelin. "If you undertook the same enquiry in Great Britain, Germany, the United States and Russia you would come out with nothing but other national idiosyncracies."

Undaunted by his critics, Gauquelin tested 25,000 Dutch, German, Italian, and Belgian horoscopes. The results backed up the French ones, and experiments with new professional groups produced further confirmation. In the horoscopes of 3142 military men either Mars or Jupiter was in a significant position. Politicians and athletes were also linked with Mars, scientists with Saturn, and actors with Jupiter. The odds against these links occurring simply by chance ranged from between one million and 50 million to one. From doctors to artists, every one of the test groups showed that planetary positions were related to profession—and in just the way astrology had always claimed. Statisticians were finally forced to take Gauquelin's results seriously.

Counter-experiments were performed in which Gauquelin's methods were applied to random groups of men and women who did not have a profession in common. In every case these random groups produced results in accordance with the laws of chance. This so impressed a number of Gauquelin's opponents that they withdrew their criticism of his work.

Gauquelin has carried out more than 20 years of statistical research in astrology, but his results should not be overestimated. He has neither proved the truth of every astrological doctrine, nor found that astrological predictions can be completely trusted. What he has shown is that there is a definite relationship between the positions of planets at the moment of birth and the profession a person chooses to follow. This is, of course, in complete accord with traditional astrological beliefs.

What about all the other details that an experienced astrologer claims to be able to detect from a person's horoscope? Has any serious research been carried out on the accuracy of horoscopes as a whole? Not enough, by any means, but sufficient to provide a strong case for further investigation.

Hans Bender, Professor of Psychology at the German University of Freiburg, has been one of the few academics to carry out scientific research in this field. As early as 1937 Professor Bender began to make experiments in "blind diagnosis," in which an astrologer is given an anonymous horoscope with no other information about the person to whom it belongs. The professor then compared the astrologer's findings with known facts about the life and character of the individual concerned. The results of these early tests were inconclusive, and in 1944–45

Bender made more extensive experiments with the astrologer and psychologist Thomas Ring. Their findings were promising and, when World War II had ended, Bender decided to continue the tests on an even larger scale.

Bender tested more than 100 astrologers, using blind diagnosis and another procedure known as "matching." For the matching tests each astrologer was given detailed notes on the lives, personalities, and appearance of up to half a dozen unidentified individuals and an equal number of horoscopes. Their task was to match up the horoscopes with the right individuals.

Results from the matching tests were confusing and unsatisfactory. The findings from blind diagnosis were more rewarding. A large number of the astrologers made statements about the individuals whose horoscopes they had examined which were true, but would be true of almost anybody. A smaller number, however, produced specific statements that were impressively and minutely accurate. Interestingly enough, these astrologers were able to justify each of their statements in terms of the astrological tradition. This made it less likely that their success was due to clairvoyance or to some other psychic gift rather than skill in their art.

Bender continued his investigations with this smaller group. He found that one particular astrologer, Walter Boer, excelled in one type of matching test as well as blind diagnosis. The particular matching test involved written records about two groups of people—one psychologically maladjusted and one normal. The records were locked in a safe to which Boer had no access, and he was given no details about the people concerned except the dates, times, and places of their birth. In a high number of cases he was able to match the psychological conclusions about these people with their horoscopes.

In 1960 American psychologist Vernon Clark carried out even more rigorous tests of this kind. Clark first selected the horoscopes of 10 people, five men and five women, each of them of a

Above: Michel Gauquelin, French scientist who started his investigation into astrological theories to disprove them. He distrusted the statistical evidence that already existed because it had been compiled from samples he thought were too small to be significant. In spite of his initial skepticism, his results showed that the classic astrological theories appeared to have been scientifically vindicated.

Below: the planetary correlation to vocational success as worked out by Gauquelin. He chose for his sample subjects eminent members of each profession since, if the astrological theory were valid, the planetary position would favor success in the chosen field.

FRE-QUENCY	♂ MARS			♃ JUPITER			♄ SATURN			☽ MOON	
HIGH	Scientists	Athletes	Physicians, Businessmen	Military Men	Politicians	Actors	Scientists	Physicians	Politicians	Authors	
AVERAGE	Politicians	Actors		Painters	Musicians		Military Men	Politicians		Scientists, Painters	Physicians, Musicians
LOW	Authors	Painters	Musicians	Scientists	Physicians		Actors	Painters	Authors	Military Men	Athletes
KEY	⚗ Scientists	👟 Athletes	🧴 Physicians	💼 Businessmen	🚢 Military Men	🎨 Painters	🎵 Musicians	🎭 Actors	🏵 Politicians	✒ Authors	

Above: Thomas Ring, well-known German astrologer. He worked with Prof. Hans Bender on a series of tests in which he predicted the life and character of a subject of whom he knew nothing except the birth facts on a horoscope.

Above right: Ernst Meier, Swiss astrologer. He is working with Bender at the Institute for the Study of Borderland Areas of Psychology and Mental Health in further attempts to provide some scientific information on the validity of astrological theory.

different profession. They were a musician, an accountant, a herpetologist (an expert on snakes), a veterinary surgeon, a teacher, an art critic, a puppeteer, a pediatrician, a librarian, and a prostitute. Clark then gave the horoscopes and a separate list of the professions to 20 astrologers and asked them to match up the two. As a control, he gave the same information to a group of 20 psychologists and social workers. The control group came out with the number of correct answers that could be expected to be obtained by chance. The astrologers produced far better results—a hundred to one against them being the result of chance.

Clark remembered, however, that 100 to one shots sometimes romp home, as anyone who plays the horses knows. He also realized that he had to make sure that the results were not due to the astrologers being psychics, unconsciously practicing some form of ESP.

The next series of tests was therefore designed to reduce the possibility of ESP to a minimum. Each of 23 astrologers was given 20 horoscopes divided into 10 pairs. With these were 10 sets of biographical data, one for each of the 10 pairs. The astrologers were told that *one* of each pair of horoscopes corresponded to the biographical data given for that pair. The

Above: Karsten Kroenke, German astrologer who specializes in astrological predictions on a commercial basis and works for industry and business. For many astrologers' clients, scientific research is interesting but not strictly relevant. What keeps most of them paying astrologers' fees is that the service seems to work.

other horoscope of each pair, they were assured, pertained to someone of the same sex and approximate age, but with a different personal history. In fact these second horoscopes were fakes, prepared for imaginary people. This was the course taken to diminish as much as possible the chances of ESP being involved.

The task of the astrologers was to fit each set of biographical data to the correct one of each of the pairs of horoscopes. Once again the results were good—100 to one against them being the result of chance. This result seemed to prove the possibility of astrological prediction. For if Clark's test astrologers could successfully decide on the basis of a horoscope which person had suffered, say, a broken leg, they could in theory have predicted that broken leg by looking at the same horoscope before the accident happened.

Clark undertook a third test, which again involved the astrologers being given pairs of horoscopes. This time one of each pair pertained to someone who had cerebral palsy. The other, a similar chart, referred to a highly gifted individual. The astrologers had to decide which of these horoscopes belonged to which of the two individuals.

Once more the results were impressive, and the odds were again 100 to one against them being the result of chance. The odds against the figures for the three experiments together being the result of chance were over a million to one. Clark's experimental findings were examined by statisticians, who found his mathematical techniques to be faultless.

What was Clark's own conclusion? "Never again," he said, "will it be possible to dismiss the astrological technique as a vague, spooky, and mystical business—or as the plaything of undisciplined psychics—or as merely the profitable device of unscrupulous quacks. Those who, out of prejudice, wish to do so will have to remain silent or repeat these experiments for themselves."

So there is evidence that astrology works. But if so, how? There have been many attempts to give a scientific answer to this question. The best known of these is the theory suggested by the psychologist Carl G. Jung.

Jung believed in what he called "synchronicity," or the meaningful coincidence. Synchronicity, said Jung, is the other side of cause and effect. In other words, if two events happen at the same time, or shortly after one another, they may be related because one event caused the other. Alternatively neither event may have caused the other, yet the two may still be linked in a meaningful way.

In the case of astrology this would mean that the Sun, Moon, and other cosmic influences do not cause particular events, but they synchronize, or coincide meaningfully with those events. According to Jung's theory, it is not the particular planetary aspects at birth that *cause* an individual to be, say, short-lived. It is merely that these aspects *coincide* with the birth of short-lived people.

An imaginary example may help to make this concept clearer. A man feels hungry and eats a meal at the same time every evening. Each evening as he begins to feel hungry the hands of the

For all the statistical evidence backing up astrologers' claims, there remain wide areas of great variation and interpretation, and there is no doubt that what one astrologer may see in a horoscope may not be what another astrologer considers to be so clearly obvious. Left: Ann Bayer, a reporter who consulted seven New York astrologers and a computer to check on the consistency of astrological interpretation. She did not come to any conclusion in her report.

Above: Linda Goodman, author of a best-selling book on astrology, said Ann Bayer must resist an ever-present temptation to live abroad, or she would lose all the good influences in her horoscope. She was also prone to develop colic, dry mouth, and loss of voice. Right: Al Morrison, past president of the Astrologers' Guild of America, differed from the others in insisting that Miss Bayer's ascendant sign was Gemini, not Scorpio. Part of his evidence was her Mickey Mouse watch. "All Gemini risings love them," he said.

Above: Keith Clayton has taught at the Inner Vision School in New York. After considering Ann Bayer's horoscope, he said that she was destined to become a foreign correspondent and travel all over the world—without being troubled by a single injury. However, he warned her of possible injury to her thighs in the near future. Clayton guided himself by the stars to give up smoking.

electric clock in his apartment always indicate that the time is 7 p.m. But it is not the position of the clock hands that produces the hunger, nor the hunger that affects the clock hands. There is no causal relationship between the two. But there is a synchronistic relationship—both the hunger and the clock time reflect the 24-hour period of the Earth's rotation.

Applying this example to astrology, the planetary positions are the "hands of the clock," and the inborn characteristics and destiny of a person born under those positions are the "feelings of hunger." Neither is the cause of the other, but both reflect some vast cosmic cycle of which we know nothing.

Curiously enough, the theory of synchronicity is almost as ancient as astrology itself, although Jung thought he had invented it. Sophisticated astrologers have adhered to it for centuries, although they have expressed it differently. The way they put it is that "the planets and the signs of the zodiac are symbols of cosmic forces, and the patterns they form synchronize with events on Earth."

Totally different theories have, however, been put forward by some modern scientists to explain the results they have obtained when studying cosmic influences. Dr. Frank A. Brown, famous for his experiments on biological clocks, has suggested that a "trigger mechanism" may account for the rhythms found in the opening of oyster shells and the activity of rats. The Moon and the Sun, Brown suggests, supply an extremely minute amount of some unknown energy to each living organism. In spite of its smallness, this energy is enough to pull a biological trigger within the organism, setting off a chain reaction that ultimately leads to the organism expending a large amount of energy.

Brown's theory is, of course, thoroughly scientific, being expressed in terms of cause and effect. However, there is no more evidence for the existence of either the trigger or the energy that supposedly sets it off than there is for the existence of the "internal clocks" that Brown had previously rejected.

Another explanation of planetary influences has been put forward by Michel Gauquelin, who worked on the relationship between horoscopes and professions. His latest theory arose from a five-year study of 30,000 parents and children during which he discovered that children tend to be born under the same, or similar, planetary positions as their parents were. We inherit our horoscopes, Gauquelin suggests, in the same way that we inherit other genetic factors. Some element in our genetic makeup is sensitive to a certain set of cosmic influences, helping to determine when we are born and affecting the future course of our lives, including our probable choice of the profession we will follow.

Of the prevailing theories, synchronicity—the idea that the positions of the planets do not cause things to happen but merely coincide with those happenings—is still the most popular explanation of how astrology works, and the one to which most astrologers adhere.

In a sense all such theories take second place to two important facts. Cosmic influences have been shown to exist, and astrology—the art of interpreting those influences—can be made to work. This even extends to predicting future events.

3

The Power of Prediction

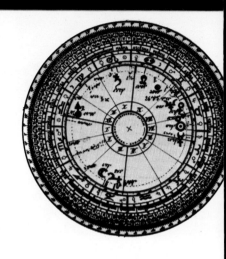

It was the evening of November 8, 1939. The main speaker and some of his close associates had left the Munich meeting hall unexpectedly early, but the platform was still crowded with minor dignitaries. In the body of the hall the audience smoked, drank beer, chatted, and laughed. Suddenly there was an ear-splitting roar as the shock wave from an explosion swept through the rooms. For a while all was confusion. The smoke- and dust-laden air masked the cries of the wounded, and the failure of the lights hampered the efforts of their would-be rescuers. When lights were finally brought and some sort of order restored, the extent

A general German preoccupation with astrology between the World Wars has led many to speculate on Hitler's attitude and receptivity to astrological predictions. His close associate Heinrich Himmler, head of the secret police, was certainly an avid occultist, but to what extent he influenced Hitler with his enthusiasms is debatable. Above: Hitler's birth chart, drawn up by Himmler's personal astrologer Wilhelm Wulff. In an analysis long after World War II, Wulff pointed out that Hitler's horoscope—with a Libra ascendant and Uranus rising—suggests unrest and catastrophe. Another configuration of Venus, Gemini, and Taurus shows Hitler's end in suicide with his woman friend. Right: a portrait of Adolf Hitler in honor of his 50th birthday in 1939, which was a crucial year.

"Himmler was a devotee of the occult..."

of the damage became apparent. The speaker's platform, where the explosion had occurred, was completely wrecked. Although the rest of the hall had suffered lightly, seven men lay dead and more than another 60 were injured, some of them severely.

The meeting that ended with such fatal suddenness on that November evening had been held to celebrate the 16th anniversary of Hitler's *Putsch*—his attempt to overthrow the German government—in 1923. That had also taken place in Munich. And the man who had escaped almost certain death by leaving early was none other than Adolf Hitler himself.

By 1939 Hitler and the Nazis had been in power for six years. Throughout the years of their rule the memory of the unsuccessful *Putsch* was kept alive. Hitler's followers who had fallen in 1923 were given the status of political martyrs, and on each anniversary of their death the Nazi "old fighters" gathered in beer halls all over Germany. Officially their purpose was to mourn their fallen comrades, but in reality they drank, gossiped over old times, and listened to speeches from their leaders.

The most notable of these annual meetings took place in Munich itself at the Bürgerbräu Beer Cellar on November 8, 1939. It was well known that Hitler would head the celebration, and the would-be assassin had placed his bomb carefully on a pillar right behind the speaker's platform. Was it just chance that caused Hitler to leave before the bomb exploded, or did he have some foreknowledge of the assassination attempt?

It has been suggested that this attempt on Hitler's life was a put-up job. The man who constructed and installed the bomb was Georg Elser. He was arrested and later died in a concentration camp. However, some people allege that Elser was the tool of a group of Gestapo men who were anxious to rid themselves of rivals in the Nazi party. It is said that Hitler himself was a party to the plot, and that he left the gathering earlier than expected in order to avoid the explosion he knew was coming.

Such a scheme would certainly have been in keeping with Hitler's known ruthlessness. However, all the evidence indicates that Hitler genuinely believed Elser to be the agent of a group of conspirators, probably inspired by British intelligence agents.

Hitler was backed up in this view by Heinrich Himmler, sinister chief of the Nazi secret police—and for a most extraordinary reason. Himmler was a devotee of the occult, and had sought the advice of a psychic in trying to find the person responsible for the bombing. He went to a *psychometrist*—a type of medium who is alleged to sense events associated with particular objects simply by touching or being near them. Himmler gave the psychometrist some fragments of the bomb mechanism to examine. She held these to her head, went into a trance, and claimed to see visions of the individuals behind the explosion. These were a group of men talking to someone named Otto. Himmler believed that this Otto could be none other than Otto Strasser, an old associate of Hitler's. He had broken with the Führer in 1930 and become leader of an underground anti-Nazi group called the Black Front.

Hitler was not unduly impressed by this medium's revelations, but he does seem to have been surprised and alarmed by a prediction of the explosion made some days before the event by the astrologer Karl Ernst Krafft.

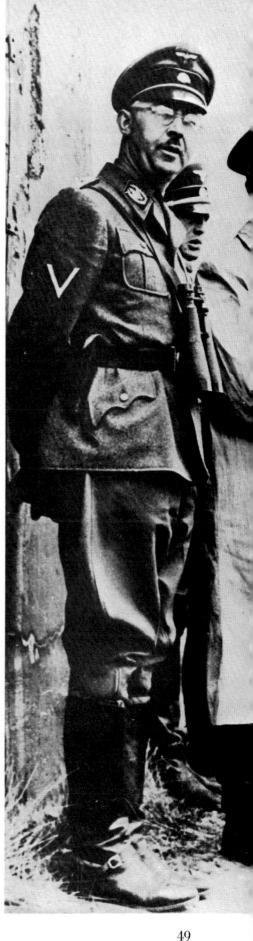

Above: the ruins of the Munich meeting hall after the bombing on November 8, 1939, in an apparent assassination attempt on Hitler. Right: Heinrich Himmler. After the Munich bombing he went to a medium to identify those responsible for the attack. She "saw" a man called Otto, whom Himmler believed was an old associate of Hitler's. In fact, the would-be bomber was named Georg Elser. Below: Himmler with the top echelon of the SS, planning their investigation in the wake of the November attempt to kill Hitler.

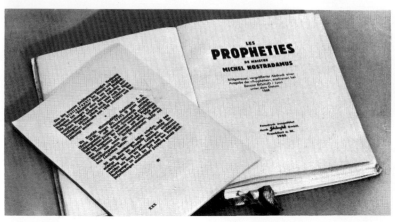

Above: Karl Ernst Krafft, the Swiss astrologer who early in November 1939 reported to Himmler's intelligence service that Hitler would be in particular danger between the 7th and 10th of that month. When his prophecy was spectacularly proved true, he came to the attention of the Third Reich leaders, including Hitler himself, and was brought in for questioning by the Gestapo. He managed to convince them that his eerie preknowledge had been acquired solely through strictly traditional astrological methods.

Above right: Krafft's facsimile edition of the prophecies of Nostradamus which he produced for Joseph Goebbels' propaganda ministry. In it Krafft assembled a few of the ambiguous quatrains with interpretations that pointed to imminent and complete Nazi victory over all opponents.

Krafft was a Swiss astrologer who had moved to Germany shortly before the outbreak of war in September 1939. Some say he was pro-Nazi and others that he was not. In any case he had personal contacts with a number of officials of Himmler's intelligence service. It was to one of these, Dr. Heinrich Fesel, that Krafft sent his prediction on November 2, 1939. He reported that Hitler's horoscope indicated that he would be in great danger in the period November 7 to 10, and that there was the "possibility of an assassination by the use of explosive material."

As soon as Krafft heard of the fulfillment of his prophecy he sent a telegram to Rudolf Hess, Hitler's deputy, drawing attention to his prediction. This telegram, Krafft was to write later, "exploded like a second bomb in Berlin." Dr. Fesel was ordered to hand over Krafft's original report, and by the morning of November 9 it was in the hands of Hitler. He was apparently impressed by its amazing accuracy.

The following day Krafft was brought to Berlin for interrogation by the Gestapo in the belief that his foreknowledge of the bomb must mean that he had been involved in the plot against Hitler's life. However, in demonstrating the exact astrological rules that had led him to his conclusions, Krafft managed to convince the Gestapo that astrology enabled its practitioners to make accurate forecasts of future events.

As a result, Krafft was employed to carry out astrological work of a political nature for the SS (Hitler's special police), the Nazi Propaganda Ministry, and even the Foreign Office. As in the 17th century, astrology was once again to be used as a means of psychological warfare, aimed at boosting the morale of the home country and demoralizing the enemy. During World War II both sides used the prophecies of the 16th-century French astrologer and seer Nostradamus to predict the defeat of the other. Krafft did some detailed research on the prophecies of Nostradamus, and this work was used by the Propaganda Ministry for their ends. He also prepared leaflets based on other ancient occult documents that could be interpreted to prophesy a German victory. In addition, he regularly cast horoscopes of the leading enemies of Nazism, such as Britain's Winston Churchill.

In the course of his work for the government Krafft made contact with a number of leading Nazis whom he converted to a belief in astrology. Among them were Robert Ley, leader of the Labor Front—the Nazi equivalent of the AFL–CIO—and Dr.

Hans Frank, "the butcher of Warsaw," Hitler's brutal governor of occupied Poland. It was to these men that Krafft made another surprisingly accurate prediction in the spring of 1940. Far from continuing to forecast German victory as his Nazi masters might have wished, Krafft foretold serious trouble. He produced a *dynogram*—an astrological forecast expressed in the form of a graph—which showed a pessimistic view of Germany's future. The dynogram indicated that Germany would meet with one military success after another until the winter of 1942–43. After that, said Krafft, the astrological indications became decidedly unfavorable, and Germany would be well advised to make peace before the end of 1942. Frank assured Krafft that the war would be over long before then.

In fact, of course, it wasn't—and in January 1943 the German armies met with the military disaster of Stalingrad, which was a turning point of the war.

Unpopular though Krafft's forecast was with the Germans, it was a demonstration once again that astrological techniques could produce accurate predictions of future events. Indeed, before his involvement with the Nazis, Krafft had come up with some even more surprising prophecies. They were made as a result of an experiment in blind diagnosis which he undertook early in 1938. Krafft had been asked to forecast the future of two individuals simply on the basis of the planetary positions at the time of their birth, without knowing who these people were or any other information about them.

Krafft declared that the first of these two people had a schizoid personality, that he was partly Jewish, and that he was unlikely to be alive after November 1938.

The second person, he said, occupied a position of authority and eminence, but would be unlikely to retain it after September 1940.

Krafft's predictions proved perfectly correct. The subject of the first blind diagnosis was Cornelius Codreanu, the half-Jewish leader of a Rumanian political movement called the Iron Guard. He was shot dead on November 30, 1938. The second person was Rumania's King Carol, who was forced to abdicate in favor of his son on September 6, 1940.

Below: one of Krafft's remarkably accurate predictions came as a result of an experiment in which he was given samples of handwriting and birth data of two men, but no further details. He predicted that one of them enjoyed a position of considerable authority, but would experience a disastrous reversal of fortune in or about September of 1940. The subject was King Carol of Rumania, pictured with his son on a state visit. He was forced to abdicate on September 6, 1940.

In spite of his undoubted abilities as an astrologer Krafft fell from favor with the Nazi leadership in the spring of 1941. Along with many other German astrologers, he was arrested and imprisoned. This seemingly abrupt change in the Nazi attitude toward astrology arose from a most unusual incident. In May 1941 Rudolf Hess, deputy leader of the Nazi Party, took a fighter plane, flew it to Scotland, and attempted to open peace negotiations with the British. Hess, who was generally believed to be under the influence of astrologers, had an astrologer on his staff. It was thought that astrological charts indicating that he was destined to make peace between Germany and Britain had persuaded him to undertake his extraordinary action. Whether or not this was true—and Hess's astrologer, naturally enough, denied it—fears had been growing for some time that astrology was exerting undue political influence in Germany. The Hess incident gave the Gestapo the ideal opportunity to move against the astrologers. It also provided a scapegoat to blame for Hess's action.

The British interned Hess. They made little use of his flight for propaganda purposes, but the incident had seriously alarmed Hitler and the other Nazi leaders. They rounded up amateur and professional astrologers, banned the public practice of astrology, suppressed all astrological magazines, and strictly forbade all astrological speculation about the future course of the war.

Nevertheless, the Nazis continued to make use of the astrologers they were so busily persecuting. So it was that after a year in solitary confinement, Karl Krafft was transferred to a Propaganda Ministry building. He was forced to produce an astrological analysis slanted against President Franklin Roosevelt and designed for political warfare purposes. In it Krafft distorted astrological principles in an attempt to prove that the president and his wife were no more than puppets of Wall Street and "international Jewry." Krafft had evidently been promised that if his work met with the approval of his Nazi masters, he would earn his release. However, it soon became apparent that the promise would not be kept, and after a few months Krafft refused to collaborate any further with his jailers. He was then interned in a concentration camp for two years. He was due to be transferred to the notorious camp at Buchenwald when he died in January 1945.

Meanwhile the authorities in Britian were also endeavoring to use astrology to aid the war effort. Britain's military leaders had not been converted to a belief in the "science of the stars," but they had come to believe that Hitler employed an astrologer to advise him, and that he might be making at least some of his political and military moves in accordance with astrological indications.

This idea had first been suggested by Virgil Tilea, the Rumanian Ambassador to London. Tilea had once met Krafft in Switzerland, and had been impressed by the astrologer's skills as a prophet. During 1940, well before Krafft was arrested, Tilea wrote to him and asked him to make a forecast of coming events. Krafft showed the letter to Dr. Fesel, his contact in the intelligence service, and asked him how he could get a reply through to London. Fesel immediately saw the possibility of using Krafft's

Above: the crashed remains of the Messerschmitt 110 in which Rudolf Hess flew to Scotland in a bizarre peace mission in 1941. He hoped to persuade Britain to give Germany a free hand against the Soviet Union in exchange for a peace settlement between them. It was suggested that this idea came from an astrologer whom Hess had on his personal staff, and the Gestapo took the opportunity of the fiasco to suppress astrology in Germany by burning most of the books and imprisoning astrologers.

Left: Rudolf Hess. In 1941 he was deputy Führer, although he had slid into the background of the Nazi leadership since 1939. He was certainly neurotic, and passionately attached to Hitler. He was found guilty at his trial in Nürnberg, and sentenced to life imprisonment. Now nearly 80 years old, he is the last Nazi leader still imprisoned—the only inmate of Berlin's Spandau prison.

Right: the Duke of Hamilton, the British aristocrat through whom Hess thought he might be able to arrange a peace treaty. He had met Hess only briefly at the Berlin Olympics in 1936, and this seemed to be all Hess went on in selecting him as a go-between.

forecast as a political weapon. He and the other security chiefs promised to get a letter to London provided they could dictate its contents. Krafft tried to drop the affair, even attempting to resign his post, but a forecast was nevertheless prepared and despatched to Virgil Tilea.

The fact that the forecast came from Berlin and seemed such an obvious piece of political propaganda convinced Tilea that Krafft was in the pay of the Nazis—perhaps even of Hitler himself— and he alerted the British authorities accordingly. If Hitler was employing an astrologer, he argued, it would be only wise for Britain to do the same. Then their astrologer could "predict the predictions" of his Nazi counterpart, and possibly anticipate Hitler's moves.

The first problem for the British was to find an astrologer sufficiently well acquainted with the techniques used by the Nazi astrologers, particularly Krafft. This was essential if the Nazi forecasts were to be anticipated correctly. Sir Orme Sargent, a high official of Britain's Foreign Office, approached a number of British astrologers. None of them, however, felt sure of using the same procedures as those employed in Berlin. It was Virgil Tilea who finally found a willing astrologer capable of doing the job. He was Hungarian-born Louis de Wohl, a partly Jewish refugee from Nazi persecution who had lived in London since 1935.

Within a short time de Wohl was head of the newly created Psychological Research Bureau, an organization which, in spite of its all-embracing title, was concerned exclusively with astrology. Throughout 1940 and the first half of 1941 the Bureau produced a stream of reports for the British Admiralty and the War Office. These included astrological analyses of the course of the war, of Hitler's probable political and military moves, and of the future careers of Nazi leaders and their allies. They were often amazingly accurate. In 1941, for example, de Wohl examined the horoscope of the Italian dictator Benito Mussolini and correctly predicted his "violent and sudden end" in 1945 at the hands of the partisans.

At this stage of the war, however, Britain's position seemed desperate. Almost all of Europe was either under German occupation or ruled by pro-Nazi governments. Hitler's armies were gaining victory after victory over the Soviet Union. The United States was still neutral and seemed likely to remain so. To many Americans, including Joseph Kennedy, father of the future president, it seemed that a German victory was inevitable.

The Nazi propaganda machine did everything in its power to convince American public opinion that this was indeed the case. No channel of communication was neglected—not even American astrological magazines. Through German agents and native-born Americans who sympathized with the Nazis, astrological forecasts prophesying a speedy German victory were planted in many American occult publications.

De Wohl's task was to ensure the publication of counter-propaganda predictions with a pro-allied content. He drew up astrological analyses that appeared in magazines from Los Angeles to Lagos, Nigeria. At a later stage of the war de Wohl also prepared "black propaganda"—information based on as-

Above: Louis de Wohl, a German astrologer who was part Jewish. He came to London in 1935. He was hired by the British for counter-propaganda, the idea being that if the Nazis were using astrology to plan tactics, it would be useful to have a line on what the Nazi astrologers would be advising.

Below: a cover of *Der Zenit*, a fake German astrological magazine which de Wohl edited in London in 1943. It was then infiltrated into Germany. The timing of printing was carefully planned so that the pessimistic predictions of U-boat disasters might appear to have been fulfilled: it was done when British intelligence received reports of the sinkings. There was an authentic *Zenit* published before the war, and great pains were taken to make the fake appear authentic.

trology that did not openly come from an allied source but appeared to originate from inside Germany itself. Under Sefton Delmer, head of British "black" political warfare, de Wohl wrote articles for fake issues of *Zenit*, a well-known prewar German astrological magazine. These were printed by skilled British forgers in a brilliant imitation of a German typeface, and smuggled into Germany from Sweden.

Despite the Nazi ban on astrological publications, these issues of the phony *Zenit* achieved a surprisingly widespread circulation inside Germany. They played a part in sapping the morale of both the civilian population and members of the armed forces. The submariners who went to sea in Germany's U-boats, for example, were hardly cheered by the predictions contained in the April 1943 issue of the false *Zenit*. Typical forecasts were: "April 4, Advisable not to go to sea if the Captain's horoscope is unfavorable; April 20, Very bad for U-boats."

Even more gloomy reading for patriotic Germans was an article in the same issue forecasting that Heinrich Himmler and other SS leaders would one day betray Hitler.

Interestingly enough, this prediction was accurately fulfilled toward the end of the war when Himmler, Schellenberg, and other trusted SS men tried to abandon the Führer and make independent arrangements with the Allies.

Below: Sefton Delmer, head of the British "black" warfare department, making a radio broadcast during World War II. Black warfare was the name given to propaganda prepared in Britain but presented as though it originated within Germany itself. De Wohl worked for Delmer's department.

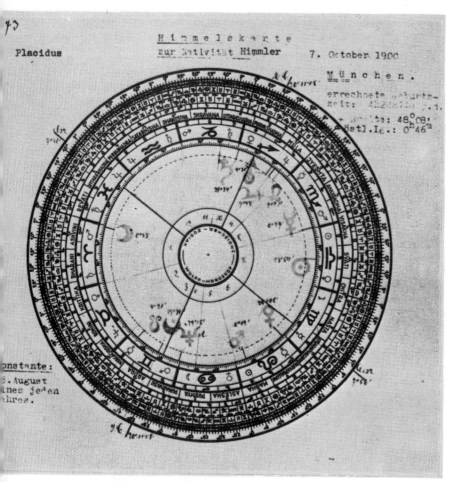

Placidus

Himmelskarte
zur Nativität Himmler   7. Oktober 1900

München.

errechnete Geburts-
zeit: ...

Left: Himmler's birth chart by Wilhelm Wulff. Unlike Krafft, who at least originally found his contact with high Nazi leaders exhilarating, Wulff was most wary of his involvement. He had the additional worry of seeing in his calculations a future that would in no way please his Nazi masters. He interpreted the chart after the war as showing that Himmler would be a commanding officer. He concluded this from the fact that Mars is in the Sixth House. The exact opposition of Saturn and Neptune foreshadowed a violent death. The favorable aspects of Jupiter could only indicate the high position he would achieve in life— it could not change the end.

Below: Himmler (at right) in Vienna in 1938. Head of the SS, he was always fascinated with unorthodox theories. There was supposed to have been a joke that one general was "worried about the stars on his epaulette and [Himmler] about the stars in his horoscope."

Himmler was himself a convinced believer in astrology—as he was in almost every form of the occult. In the later stages of the war he hardly ever made a move without consulting his favorite astrologer, Wilhelm Wulff. Far from enjoying the influence this gave him over the powerful SS chief, Wulff found his position an extremely difficult one. His astrological calculations convinced him that Germany was bound to lose the war, and that both Himmler and Hitler were destined for early and unpleasant deaths. Because he was too honest an astrologer to conceal these conclusions entirely, he consequently ran the constant risk of being thrown into a concentration camp as a "defeatist."

Himmler was so fascinated by unorthodox theories that he had formed a section of the SS exclusively devoted to them. This included a bureau for long-range weather forecasting using a combination of astrology and a strange theory of cosmic influences known as the "World Ice Theory." The theory was invented by an engineer called Hans Hörbiger. He believed that the solar system was formed when a huge block of cosmic ice fell into the Sun, causing a tremendous explosion whose effects were still continuing.

Himmler was not the only high-ranking Nazi who believed in the World Ice Theory. Its admirers included Joseph Goebbels, chief of the Propaganda Ministry, and even Hitler himself. The Führer declared that after the war he would build an observatory dedicated to "the three greatest astronomers of history"—Ptolemy, the intellectual father of modern astrology, Copernicus, the 16th-century astronomer who first put forward the theory that the Earth revolved around the Sun, and Hans Hörbiger.

Hitler's admiration for Hörbiger's theories may even have been responsible for Germany's disastrous campaign in the Soviet Union in the winter of 1941–42. Some people suggest that because of a forecast from Himmler's Hörbigerian weather bureau, which prophesied an exceptionally mild winter, Hitler failed to equip his troops adequately for the harsh Russian winter. The German soldiers had to fight in sub-zero temperatures clad only in their light summer uniforms. In addition their armor and transportation were almost totally immobilized from the cold.

Himmler became disillusioned with his weather bureau around the end of 1941, and abruptly closed it down. Moreover, there is no evidence that Hitler ever based his military moves on Hörbigerian theories, in spite of his admiration for Hörbiger. Nor did he place as much faith in astrology as some of his top advisers. He had dismissed Elsbeth Ebertin's warning about the Munich *Putsch* in 1923. Even Krafft's prediction of the bomb in the Munich Beer Cellar, and the events surrounding Rudolf Hess's flight to Scotland, do not appear to have alarmed him for long.

Only toward the end of the war when Germany's situation had become desperate is Hitler known to have taken an interest in his horoscope. In *The Last Days of Hitler*, British historian Hugh Trevor-Roper recounts how in April 1945 Joseph Goebbels and Hitler discussed Hitler's own horoscope and of the German Reich. These horoscopes, previously prepared by Himmler's special research department, had accurately predicted the outbreak of war in 1939, German victories until 1941, and the subsequent defeats and disasters until the early part of 1945. Goebbels

Nazi Occultism

Heinrich Himmler, the notorious head of the SS and one of the most powerful men in Nazi Germany, was a fanatical occultist. To pursue his interests fully and undisturbed, he obtained a ruined castle in Westphalia and made it the center of his own cult. This was a kind of paganism based on the most way-out aspects of occult subjects.

Himmler renovated the castle in handsome style, and the great banqueting hall became the center for important rites and conferences. Around a gigantic table in the hall were throne-like wooden chairs upholstered richly in pigskin. Each chair had the name of its regular occupant inscribed on a silver plate at the top. There were never more than 12 others besides Himmler, and each was a favorite of his.

Why precisely 13 around the table? Some say it was a parody of the Last Supper, others that it represented Himmler as the Sun surrounded by the zodiacal 12 signs.

Whatever the significance of the number, the 13 SS men would sit at the table both for meetings about SS business and for group meditation. In meditating they would sit in silence for many hours. Their purpose? To become more closely identified with the Aryan "race soul."

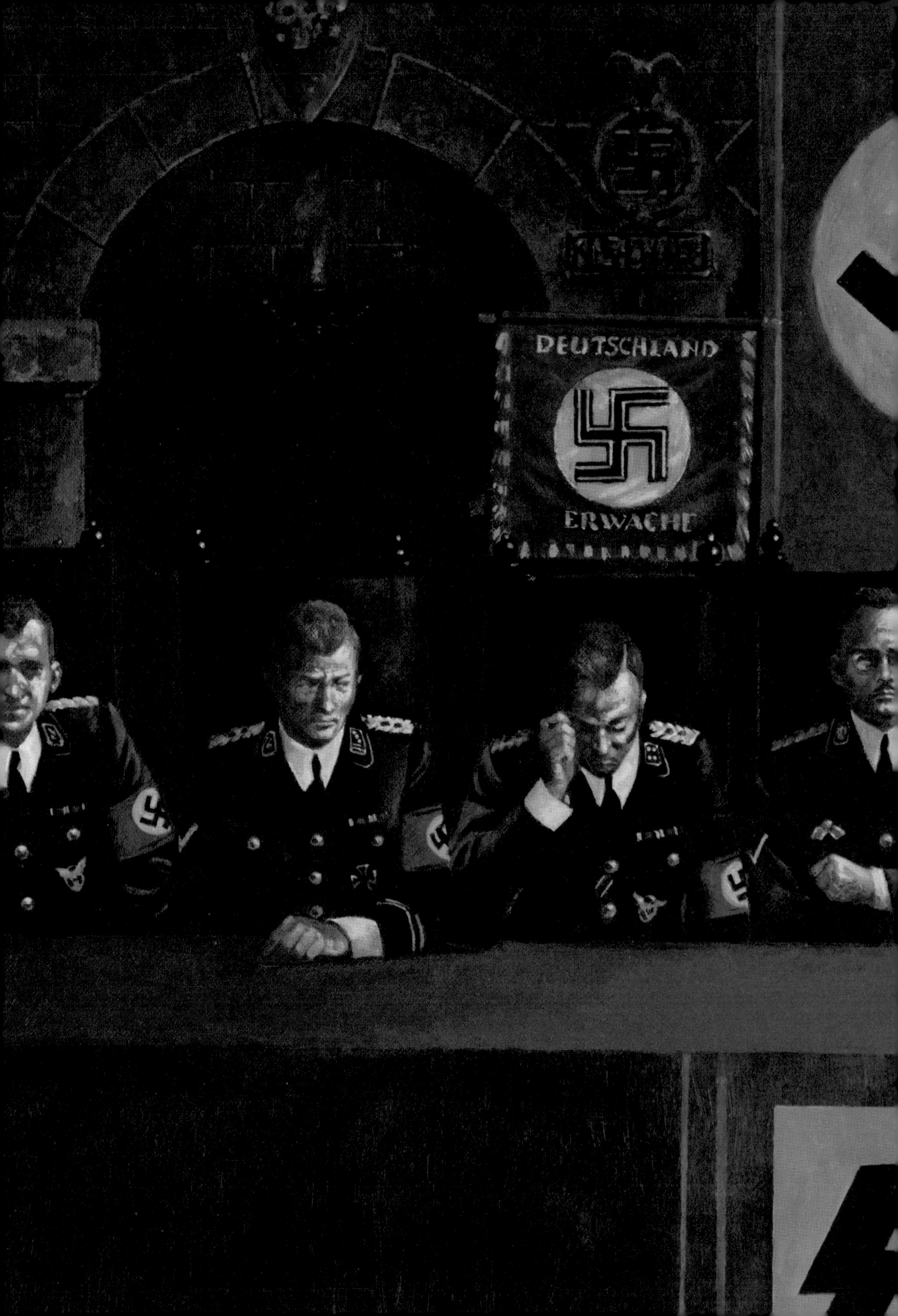
DEUTSCHLAND
ERWACHE

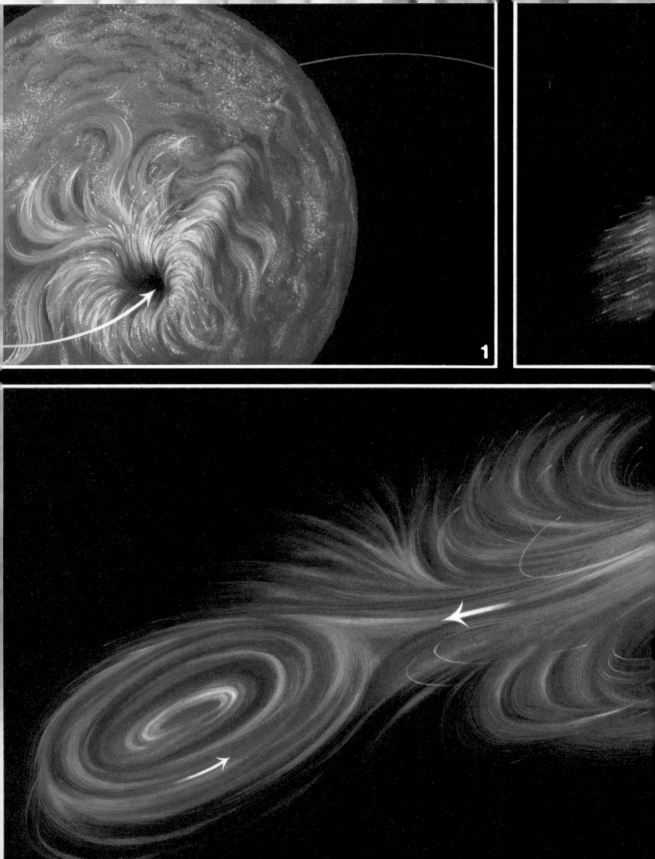

1

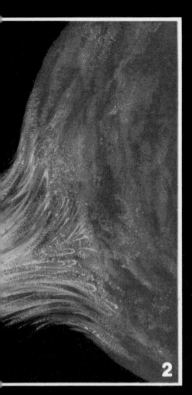

was, however, delighted to report that the horoscopes pointed to an overwhelming German victory at the end of April 1945, followed by peace in August. Two weeks later Goebbels and Hitler were both dead. On May 8, Germany surrendered to the Allies.

Throughout the war, the astrologers who worked for the Nazis walked the dangerous path between security and arrest, based on their collaboration. On the allied side, de Wohl, who knew nothing of Krafft's imprisonment, faced the problem of deciding how much the Nazi astrologers would dare to tell their master. Nevertheless, the well-authenticated accuracy of many of the predictions made by astrologers such as Krafft, Wulff, and de Wohl, even under extraordinary circumstances, is viewed by some as positive proof of astrology's validity. Others would say that such successful predictions are due only to coincidence, and would point to the human tendency to remember prophecies that have been fulfilled and to forget those that have not.

History certainly provides many examples of both kinds of prediction. The outbreak of World War I, the Russian Revolution, the death of Britain's King Edward VII in 1910 and of Pope John XXIII in 1963 were all accurately forecast by astrologers. Predictions of the disappearance of Stalin from politics in 1946, and of revolution in Britain in 1962 were far from what happened in fact. Louis de Wohl forecast in 1938 that there would be "no war in the near future," and incorrectly prophesied that the death of the Hindu religious leader Mahatma Gandhi would be in 1939. (Gandhi did not die until 1948.) Most notorious of all is the popular and oft-repeated forecast of the end of the world. This has been prophesied for almost every century since astrology began. It still had some people scurrying for the nearest mountaintop as recently as 1962.

Prediction is without doubt the most difficult area of astrology, and predictive failures do not necessarily invalidate the art. Modern scientific investigations have suggested that astrologers can, at least in theory, predict events before they happen. Much may, of course, depend on the skill of the individual astrologer.

Whatever their success or failure, the expertise of some astrologers, and the influence which their art has exerted on history, continue to make their subject a fascinating one. And in spite of the skeptics, people are likely to go on searching the heavens—not only for clues to our future but also for an understanding of our past.

4

Earth in Chaos

Men choked to death in the suffocating black smoke that shrouded the Earth. Volcanoes erupted, the sea boiled in places, and the land was shaken by earthquakes. Showers of vermin and bloodlike liquid rained from the sky. The very rotation of our planet on its axis first slowed down and then stopped, so that the Sun appeared to stand still in the sky.

These and other vast catastrophes took place well within historic times—and they were caused by cosmic influences. So says the unorthodox scholar Dr. Immanuel Velikovsky. He backs up his claims with evidence from Greek poetry, from Egyptian papyrus manuscripts, from the Old Testa-

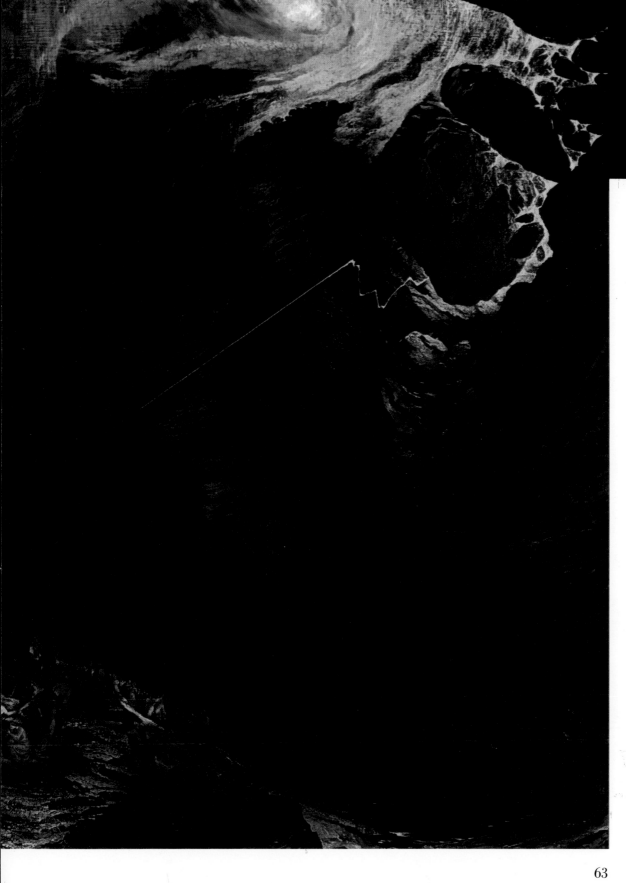

"Velikovsky's... ideas have compelled the attention of ...scientists"

ment, and from many other sources among ancient literature.

The astrologer looks for cosmic influences that mark events in the here and now—or those that may occur in the future. Velikovsky and others like him are concerned with cosmic forces that may have affected our planet in the past in such a way as to have exerted a profound influence in human history. Velikovsky's field of study is called *cosmology*—the philosophy of the origin and structure of the Universe. Although his ideas are unorthodox, they have compelled the attention of some leading modern scientists and of many interested laymen.

Velikovsky believes that, at some time between 3000 and 2000 B.C., a vast comet appeared in the outer solar system and began to head toward the Sun. The exact origin of this comet, which was eventually to become the planet Venus, is uncertain according to Velikovsky. But probably it was thrown off from the giant planet Jupiter by some titanic explosion. For this view Velikovsky quotes as evidence the Greek myth in which the goddess Athene, associated with the planet Venus, was born from the head of Zeus—the king of the gods whom the Greeks identified with the planet Jupiter. Velikovsky believes that before settling into its own orbit as Venus, the comet had several near collisions with both Mars and our own planet.

According to Velikovsky, the first of these encounters took place around 1500 B.C., and the earthly disasters to which it gave rise are recorded in the Old Testament's *Book of Exodus*. As the Earth entered the comet's tail, showers of red dust were drawn into our atmosphere, turning the Nile and other rivers to "blood." This dust gave rise to some of the biblical "plagues of Egypt," causing intense irritation to the skins of man and beast and showering the land with "vermin"—lowly forms of life either originating from the Venus comet itself or produced by sudden mutations resulting from the abnormal atmospheric conditions.

The Old Testament says that the plagues were followed by "hail, and fire mingled with the hail." Velikovsky argues that this fiery hailstorm took place when the head of the comet came closer to Earth. The hail, he says, consisted not of frozen water but of stones and meteorites thrown off by the comet. The fire "mingled with the hail" can be accounted for by supposing that the comet consisted partly of hydrocarbons, which are petroleumlike substances. When such matter rained on the Earth, it burst into flame as it came into contact with the oxygen present in the atmosphere.

Nearer and nearer came the comet until the influence of its gravitational and electromagnetic field made the Earth slow to a halt. For three days one half of the globe was in full sunlight, and the other, in which Egypt was located, was shrouded in night. In the words of the Old Testament: "there was a thick darkness in all the land of Egypt three days. They saw not one another, neither rose any from his place. . . ."

Velikovsky interprets the final biblical plague brought on the Egyptians—the "smiting of the first-born"—as a distorted account of the result of a great earthquake induced by the comet's approach. The Egyptian's suffered more heavily from the earthquake than their Israelite slaves, he says, because they lived in stone houses and their slaves dwelt in mud-plastered reed huts.

The events that took place during the Israelites' flight from Egypt, Velikovsky goes on, resulted from the continuing proximity of the comet. The parting of the Red Sea, for example, was caused by the gravitational pull of the comet on the waters of the ocean. The "pillar of smoke by day and of fire by night," which went before Moses and his followers, was the tail of the comet.

The comet finally moved away from the Earth but returned 52 years later when Joshua had succeeded Moses as leader of the Israelites. Once again there were worldwide catastrophes. The Sun stood still, and great showers of stones fell from the sky. Everywhere there were floods, earthquakes, and volcanic eruptions. Some of these events, says Velikovsky, are recorded in the tenth chapter of the *Book of Joshua.*

After this second major encounter with the comet, the Earth and its planetary neighbors enjoyed celestial peace for almost 700 years. After that the planet Mars had several near collisions with the comet, and the two bodies exchanged great electrical discharges. According to Velikovsky, these encounters are recorded in the form of myth and legend in much early literature. They are described, for example, in the *Iliad*—the Greek poet Homer's

Above: the Plague of Darkness. Velikovsky interprets this as the report of what happened when the comet approached so closely that it stopped the Earth's rotation, so that for three days Egypt was in utter darkness on the far side of the Earth from the Sun.

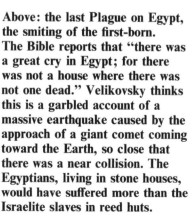

Above: the last Plague on Egypt, the smiting of the first-born. The Bible reports that "there was a great cry in Egypt; for there was not a house where there was not one dead." Velikovsky thinks this is a garbled account of a massive earthquake caused by the approach of a giant comet coming toward the Earth, so close that there was a near collision. The Egyptians, living in stone houses, would have suffered more than the Israelite slaves in reed huts.

epic poem on the war between the Greeks and Trojans. However, they are under the guise of the lengthy and violent struggles between the god Ares or Mars and the goddess Athene—the Venus comet.

After these celestial "battles," Mars temporarily settled into an orbit that came dangerously close to that of the Earth every 15 years. There was a particularly close encounter between Mars and the comet in 687 B.C.—the year in which an Assyrian army besieging Jerusalem was suddenly destroyed in the night by "the Angel of Death." This angel, asserts Velikovsky, was in reality a shower of meteoric stones of Martian origin. The electromagnetic discharges resulting from the near collision jolted Mars into a new orbit around the Sun—the orbit it occupies today. At around the same time, or perhaps earlier, the comet settled into a stable orbit as the planet Venus.

Velikovsky's theories are extraordinary. To accept them requires revision of many strongly held beliefs in the fields of astronomy, history, geology, and mythology. Are orthodox scholars wrong? Did cosmic events profoundly affect our planet and the course of our history as Velikovsky believes? Is Velikovsky merely a crank, or are his theories worthy of serious examination? To answer these questions, we need to see how Velikovsky arrived at his revolutionary conclusions.

Born in Russia in 1895, Velikovsky specialized in foreign languages and mathematics at secondary school in Moscow. He graduated with first-class honors and a gold medal. Subsequently, he studied the natural sciences and medicine at Moscow's Free University, at Montpellier in France, and at the University of Edinburgh in Scotland.

In 1921 he moved to Berlin where he practiced medicine and, in collaboration with Professor Loewe, began publication of a series of scientific monographs under the overall heading of *Scripta Universitatis*. The volume on mathematical physics in this series was edited by Albert Einstein, the genius who developed the theory of relativity. Einstein and Velikovsky became personal friends and their friendship endured until Einstein's death. Clearly the greatest mathematical physicist of all time considered Velikovsky to be something more than a crank.

In 1923 Velikovsky emigrated to what is now the state of Israel. He remained there until 1939 except for a period spent in Vienna studying psychoanalysis under the first famous psychoanalyst Sigmund Freud. In 1939 he moved to the United States in order to carry out research on the ideas that Freud had expressed in his book *Moses and Monotheism* concerning the origin of religion.

As Velikovsky delved more deeply into the life of Moses he noted more and more puzzling gaps in the historical records. In seeking to determine the time of the Exodus—the Israelites' departure from Egypt—for example, he found that the list of Egyptian dynasties was completely jumbled. He claimed that some dynasties were duplicated in the existing records, others that were written about had never existed, and still others were displaced in time by between 500 and 800 years. Through his discoveries of gaps and errors in the scriptures, Velikovsky became convinced that around the time of the Exodus some great physical disaster had occurred. Over the next nine years he developed his

Below: a medieval miniature showing all of the appalling plagues that Egypt suffered— according to the Bible because the Pharaoh would not let the Children of Israel go. Velikovsky interprets them all as confused accounts of cosmic disasters.

67

theories concerning cosmic catastrophes and their influence on human history. He outlined his ideas and his evidence in a book entitled *Worlds in Collision*.

In 1949 the book was accepted and prepared for publication by a leading New York publishing company. They realized that Velikovsky's revolutionary interpretation of history and astronomy would arouse controversy. But they were unprepared for the intellectual storm that is reported to have burst over their heads when some prepublication extracts from the book appeared in the pages of *Harpers* magazine. Rumor has it that Velikovsky's "catastrophism" so horrified some orthodox scientists that they prevented publication of his book. They did so by approaching his publishers and warning them that if they went ahead with the publication of *Worlds in Collision*, they would bring about the withdrawal of all scientific textbooks from that publisher's list. Publication of the book was abandoned.

Another major American publisher accepted the book, however, and in 1950 *Worlds in Collision* was published. It rapidly became a best seller. It was followed by a number of works in which Velikovsky developed his controversial view of early history and presented further evidence in favor of catastrophism.

As time went on, new discoveries began to lend weight to some of the scientific heresies that Velikovsky had put forward in *Worlds in Collision*. His assertions that Venus has an extremely high surface temperature and that Mars is cratered like the Moon, for instance, have subsequently proved correct. Orthodox astronomers and other scientists found themselves forced to face up to the challenge of Velikovsky's theories.

In 1974 a major confrontation of ideas took place. At the annual meeting of the American Association for the Advancement of Science, the principal scientific society in the United States, time was devoted to a special "Velikovsky session." Opponents of the catastrophic theory met and argued face-to-face with Velikovsky himself. None of these critics was converted to Velikovsky's views, but most of them seem to have been forced to recognize Velikovsky as a major interdisciplinary scholar. He was fully able to hold his own in discussion with specialists—astronomers, geologists, and physicists—in their own particular fields of knowledge.

Dr. James Warwick, a radioastronomer from Colorado University, acknowledged that Velikovsky had correctly claimed that radio noise would be found to be coming from Jupiter—and that he had done so at a time when radioastronomers held the notion to be nonsensical. Similarly Professor Michelson of the Illinois Institute of Technology granted that Velikovsky had been right in his assertion—sneered at by orthodox scientists when it was first made—that close approaches of planet-sized bodies to one another would result in titanic electrostatic discharges. Even more interestingly, Professor Michelson agreed that if the Earth's electrical charge were removed its rotation would be stopped. He conceded that, had this happened in ancient times as Velikovsky maintained, it could have produced the plague of Egypt's three-day long darkness. It could also have resulted in the Sun's standing still at the time of Joshua.

On the other side, there is a good deal of evidence against

Above: an artist's impression of what Velikovsky says happened: a terrible fiery comet fills the sky, showering meteorites and flaming hydrocarbons down on the helpless inhabitants of the Earth. Velikovsky's explanation of the lack of clear records on such catastrophes is that the survivors repressed all memories because the experience was so overwhelming. However, the memories returned in symbolic form in the mysterious myths and allegories that puzzle us today.

Velikovsky's catastrophic theories. One example is the fact that many stalactites and stalagmites—the icicle-shaped deposits that grow down from the ceilings and up from the floors of certain caves—seem to show thousands of years of steady growth uninterrupted by cosmic disasters. Another major argument against Velikovsky is the absence of any definite documented record of the supposed catastrophes, even though they are alleged to have taken place well within historical times.

In fairness to Velikovsky it should be said that he provides an explanation for this historical deficiency. The explanation is a psychological one that he calls "collective amnesia." He argues that the experiences undergone by humanity at the time of the catastrophes were so terrible that the survivors repressed the detailed memories of what had happened. These memories returned into people's consciousness from the unconscious in the symbolic forms of the myths and legends recorded in such documents as the Old Testament and Homer's *Iliad*.

There is, then, evidence both for and against Velikovsky.

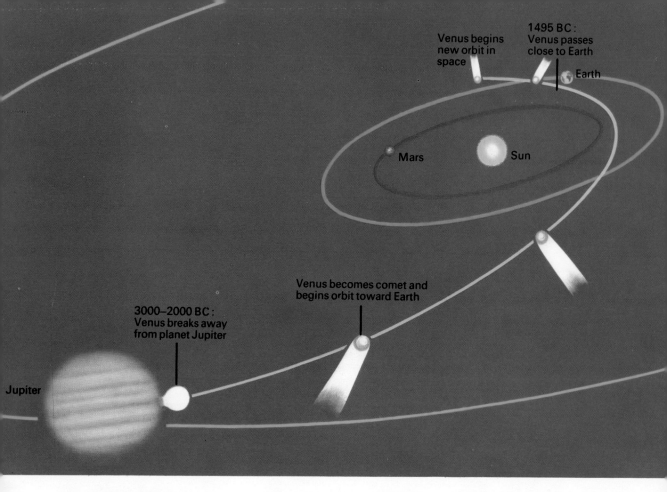

Venus begins
new orbit in
space

1495 BC:
Venus passes
close to Earth

Earth

Mars

Sun

Venus becomes comet and
begins orbit toward Earth

3000–2000 BC:
Venus breaks away
from planet Jupiter

Jupiter

**These diagrams give a picture
of Velikovsky's theories about
worlds colliding in space and
affecting Earth cataclysmically.
Above: it all starts with the
breakaway of Venus from Jupiter,
for which Velikovsky finds his
evidence in Greek myth. According
to the Greeks, Athene—who is
associated with the planet
Venus—was born from the head
of Zeus, associated with the
planet Jupiter. Later, as Venus
careered around space before
settling into an orbit, it
nearly struck Earth. At that
time came the plagues of Egypt
recorded in the Old Testament,
says Velikovsky. These included
the shower of vermin and the
three days of complete darkness.**

Perhaps the truth lies somewhere between orthodox views and
the theories of Velikovsky. For while cosmic disasters on the
scale of those described by Velikovsky seem improbable, there is
a good deal of hard evidence that the Mediterranean area was
subject to more than one large-scale devastation in historic times.
There were many floods, fires, volcanic outbreaks, and disasters
whose cause is still a matter of debate. The greatest of these
disasters took place about 1500 B.C. when the world's worst-ever
volcanic explosion ripped apart the island of Santorin between
Greece and Crete. It may even have destroyed the remarkable
civilization that existed on Crete.

Evidence of the 1500 B.C. disaster was discovered by the leading
French archeologist Professor Claude Schaeffer. In the course of
his excavations at the site of the ancient city of Ugarit in present-
day Ras Shamra on the coast of Syria, Professor Schaeffer found
that the culture of Ugarit had been completely destroyed about
that time. He also discovered that there had been four other
catastrophes on the same site—the first as far back as 3200 B.C.,
and the last around 800 B.C. What is more, Professor Schaeffer
found some indications that these calamities had been global in
scope. While his timing of historical events differed from that of
Velikovsky, he also thought there had been five worldwide devas-
tations within historic times. Moreover he also felt that these
events had possibly wiped out emerging, or even fully developed,
cultures as well as the documentary and other evidence for their
existence.

American Professor Charles Hapgood takes his belief in

Below: 1. Venus and Mars come close to colliding in the 8th century. The shocks on Earth are recorded as encounters between gods in much early literature, according to Velikovsky's theory. 2. Venus gets especially close to Mars in the 7th century. In 687 B.C. an Assyrian army is destroyed by what the Bible calls "an angel." Velikovsky asserts this was a meteoric shower from Mars. 3. Venus and Mars settle into the orbits that they occupy today.

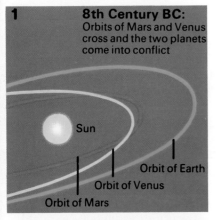

8th Century BC:
Orbits of Mars and Venus cross and the two planets come into conflict

Sun

Orbit of Earth

Orbit of Venus

Orbit of Mars

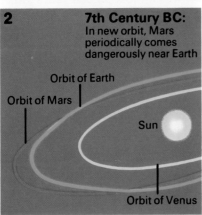

7th Century BC:
In new orbit, Mars periodically comes dangerously near Earth

Orbit of Earth

Orbit of Mars

Sun

Orbit of Venus

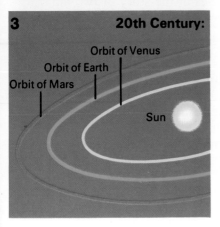

20th Century:

Orbit of Venus

Orbit of Earth

Orbit of Mars

Sun

earthly catastrophes even farther back. He maintains that major shifts in the Earth's continents destroyed one of the world's most advanced civilizations 10,000 to 15,000 years ago. And he believes that this disaster was brought about by changes in the activity of the Sun.

Professor Hapgood's idea originated from the theory of continental drift. This holds that all the world's continents were once joined together in a huge land mass but have since drifted apart, floating like giant icebergs on the Earth's shifting crust.

The theory of continental drift was first proposed in 1912 by geophysicist and meteorologist Alfred Wegener. As can be expected, it was originally greeted with widespread skepticism. As the years have passed, however, evidence has grown that the continents not only moved their positions in the past, but that they may still be drifting slowly apart today. Most geologists now accept this theory. But even if it is generally agreed that the continents do move, the problem remains of what causes that movement.

Hapgood put forward his explanation in his book *Earth's Shifting Crust*, published in 1958. It was based on the idea that there are marked variations in the amount of heat that reaches the Earth from the Sun. These variations last for a few thousand, or tens of thousands, of years—a short period in geological terms.

When the Earth is receiving its full quota of heat from the Sun, says Hapgood, there are no icecaps at the poles, the world goes happily on its way, and the amount of continental drift is very small. Then, quite suddenly, there is an unexplained reduction in the Sun's radiation, and ice begins to form at the world's poles. It would take only a relatively small decline in the Sun's output of heat for this to happen. It might also arise from cosmic influences, such as the near approach of gigantic cometlike bodies that cause minute changes in the Earth's orbit. In this case the Sun might still be producing the same amount of heat, but the alterations in the Earth's orbit would reduce the quantity of heat reaching our planet, and cause ice to form at the poles.

According to Hapgood the newly formed ice is distributed unevenly, with more ice on one side of the pole than the other. The rotation of the Earth affects these ice masses unevenly so that a centrifugal force is transmitted to the Earth's rigid crust. When the force has reached sufficient intensity, the crust slips over the Earth's inner layers, bringing the polar areas sliding with catastrophic speed toward the equator.

Hapgood believes that the last such catastrophic movement took place some 10,000 or 15,000 years ago. At that time the now icebound Antarctic was a temperate continent, probably the home of an advanced civilization. It was about 2500 miles nearer the equator than it is today. Suddenly—within a few thousand years—the Earth's crust slid thousands of miles, shifting Hudson Bay and Quebec 2500 miles southward, displacing Siberia the same distance northward, and moving the Antarctic to the South Pole.

According to Hapgood, then, a decline in the Sun's radiation or changes in the Earth's orbit caused catastrophic changes on the surface of our world in the comparatively recent past.

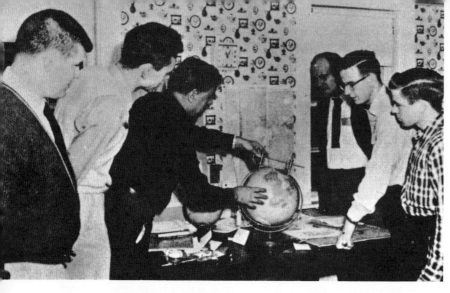

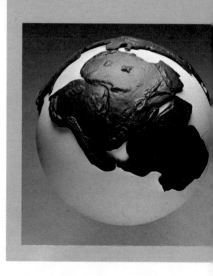

Above: Charles Hapgood (center) uses a globe in a discussion of the Piri Re'is map. In 1958 he put forward his theory that, in the distant past, certain cosmic influences affected the amount of the Sun's radiation reaching the Earth and drastically changed the Earth's surface. He also suggests that the last such catastrophe, some 10,000 or 15,000 years ago, shifted the land masses of the Southern Hemisphere to such an extent that it swiftly destroyed an advanced civilization in what is now Antarctica—then, he says, a temperate continent. Hapgood has used the Piri Re'is map as evidence to support his ideas.

Hapgood's extraordinary theory met with the approval of no less a scientist than Albert Einstein. "I am very enthusiastic about Hapgood's theory," he wrote. "His idea is original and extremely illuminating. . . . He has also offered ample material to confirm his theory. In my opinion, this astonishing, genuinely exciting thesis merits the serious attention of everyone who is concerned with the problem of the Earth's development."

Hapgood's theory supposes that major climatic changes have occurred surprisingly suddenly—and evidence is growing that this may have been so. For example, Willi Dansgaard and some of his fellow scientists at the University of Copenhagen studied an ice sample from Greenland that was almost 90,000 years old. It dated back to one of the Ice Ages to which the Earth has been subjected. From changes in the atomic composition of the ice, they found that Greenland had passed from a warm temperate climate to a full Ice Age in the space of a mere hundred years. It has been suggested that this figure is misleading, and that Dansgaard's sample had been affected by the pressures to which it had been submitted. Nevertheless, there is other independent evidence that the onset of the Ice Ages was sudden. The oak forests of Greece, for example, appear to have been destroyed abruptly, and not over a long period.

But why did Hapgood believe that, before its sudden freezing, the Antarctic had been the site of an advanced civilization, doomed to destruction by cosmic catastrophe?

The answer to this question lies in the story of two amazing maps of the world. These maps were drawn in 1513 and 1528 by a Turkish sailor named Piri Re'is on the basis of his studies of ancient documents to which he had access.

Only fragments of these maps have survived the centuries, and it was not until 1953 that they first received serious study. It was then that a Turkish naval officer sent a copy of the Piri Re'is maps to the chief engineer of the United States Navy's Hydrographical Department. The naval officer in turn showed it to Arlington H. Mallery, an expert on ancient maps.

Mallery was fascinated by the maps which were unlike any other 16th-century maps he had ever seen, and he began the task of interpreting them. Almost from the first he was joined by Charles Hapgood, and the two men worked together. Their first

The stages in the breakup of the old Southern Hemisphere according to the scientifically accepted theory of continental drift. The continents formed a single landmass 150 million years ago (far left). Then Australia, South America, and Antarctica moved away from Africa 75 million years ago. Finally the continents began to take their present positions 50 million years ago. This theory, first proposed by Alfred Wegener, was the basis for Hapgood's more unorthodox theory.

problem was to discover the system of projection—the method of reproducing the curved surface of the globe on the flat surface of a map—that Piri Re'is had used in drawing up his original charts.

Mallery and Hapgood based their work on studies carried out over the years by the Swedish scholar Nordenskjöld, an expert on 16th-century map making. Soon they were convinced that they understood both the nature of the maps' projection, and exactly what Piri Re'is had intended to portray. The result was fantastic. Not only did the maps give an accurate portrayal of the coasts of North and South America—previously believed to have been largely unknown at the time the maps were drawn—but they also appeared to show the coastal outlines of the Antarctic and of Greenland as they would be if not covered with ice.

These hidden outlines are fairly well known today. Sophisticated techniques—such as measuring the span of shock waves from controlled explosions and the vibrations produced by earthquakes originating from a known center—have enabled modern scientists to map the land that lies buried under the ice. Such techniques had not of course been developed at the time of Piri Re'is.

Could the maps be modern forgeries? To judge from variations between the Piri Re'is charts and modern maps of the Antarctic coastline, this seems unlikely. For example, the Piri Re'is maps showed islands off the coast of Antarctica where none were believed to exist. Only recently it was found that these islands coincided with mountain tops discovered beneath the ice by an international expedition to the Antarctic.

On another point, Piri Re'is showed two bays where modern maps indicated only dry land. Seismic measurements were carried out at these points with unexpected results: Piri Re'is had been correct, and modern researchers had been wrong.

The conclusions of Mallery and Hapgood are so extraordinary that they have, naturally enough, met with considerable opposition. Most of this has come from Soviet Union scholars, who have played their part in international research programs in the Antarctic. They believe that the Piri Re'is maps show the coastline of Patagonia and Tierra del Fuego rather than that of the Antarctic. However, even this solution would leave many historical questions unanswered. For when Piri Re'is made his charts, details of these areas were also unknown to Western map makers.

Mallery and Hapgood were unshaken by the Russian attacks. They remained convinced that the originals of the charts from which Piri Re'is drew his information must have been drawn up at a time when the Antarctic continent was free of ice and, still more, that the culture which produced them must have been an advanced one.

The originals of the Piri Re'is maps, they maintain, must have been made around 10,000 or 15,000 years ago by fully civilized people. "At the time when the maps were made," says Mallery, "there must have been . . . hydrographical specialists, for neither a single explorer nor even a group of explorers can make maps of continents or enormous territories, as apparently happened some thousands of years ago. It can only be done by experienced technicians. . . . I cannot understand how these maps could have been made without the help of aviation. Moreover, the degrees of longitude are absolutely accurate—something we ourselves were unable to achieve until two centuries ago."

Hapgood believes that these extraordinary maps were made by inhabitants of the Antarctic continent itself, and that buried beneath the ice lie the remnants of a once great technological civilization—a civilization possibly more advanced than our own.

Hapgood's theories, like those of Velikovsky, are unorthodox, and perhaps time alone will show whether they contain more fact than fantasy. Nevertheless, both men raise some tantalizing questions about our planet and our past; and in an area where orthodox science cannot yet provide the answers, it is just possible that some of their ideas will eventually turn out to be correct. After all, it is only now that scientists have began to discover the remarkable relationships between cosmic events and many aspects of our life on Earth—relationships that a previous generation of scientists would have dismissed as absurd. Might those influences once have had far more violent and far-reaching effects, as Velikovsky and Hapgood suggest? In unorthodox cosmology as in astrology, it may be wise to keep an open mind.

Right: the Piri Re'is map, a Turkish map on parchment dating from 1513. Hapgood believes it shows details of the Antarctic coast (at bottom) now under ice— that could only have been recorded by skilled technicians. Skeptics say that Hapgood is using a projection meant to be used only as a global projection on what is only part of the world. He then misinterprets what the map maker meant to portray—which is, they say, nothing that a skilled navigator of the period would not have been completely familiar with.

Below: Adélie Land in Antarctica, the frozen white wilderness of Earth's fifth largest continent. The winds that scream across the bleak vastness reach 200 miles per hour, and in the interior the temperature plunges to −100°F. Yet this is the place, according to Hapgood, where an advanced civilization once flourished in a temperate climate—before it was snuffed out and irretrievably buried beneath encroaching ice.

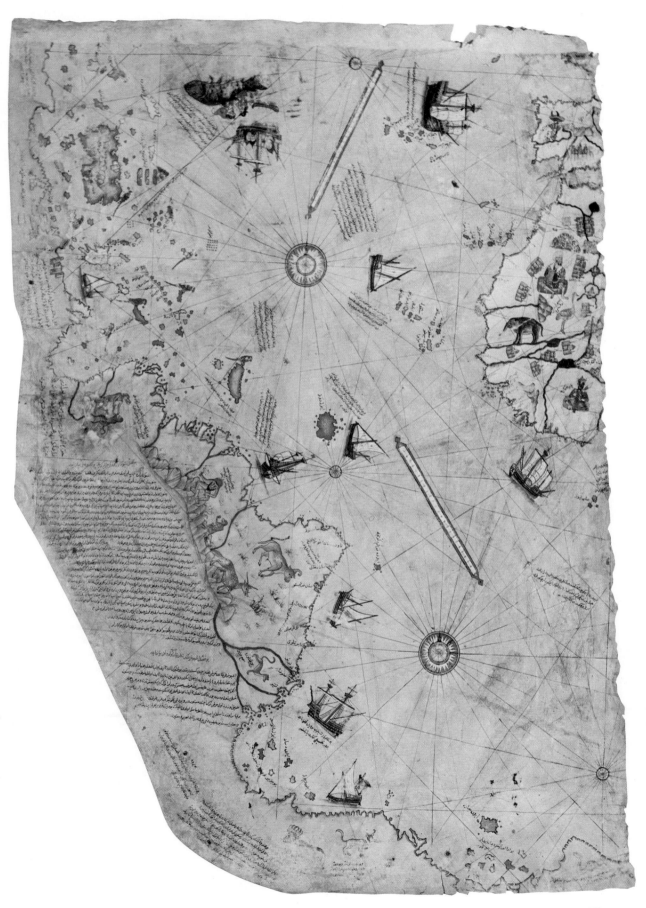

The Zodiac and You

As the Russian shells whined overhead and crashed to earth with a deafening roar, Alfred Witte hugged the half-frozen mud that formed the floor of his dugout and swore. Two minutes before, the quarter-mile corridor of snow-covered Polish landscape which separated the Russian and German armies on that clear cold day of January 1916 had been peaceful enough. Now it was a hell of exploding shell and mortar bombs, a strip of death swept by rifle and machine gun fire. Far from alarming him, however, this sudden barrage both annoyed and puzzled Witte, an enthusiastic peacetime astrologer from Ham-

Throughout the ages mankind has either firmly believed that the stars affected an individual's destiny, or suspected it. This is reflected in the astrological and magical tenet of "As above, so below" in which events in heaven are matched by responses on Earth. Right: an illustration showing the correlation of the signs of the zodiac with parts of the human body, from a German manuscript on astrology of the 14th century.

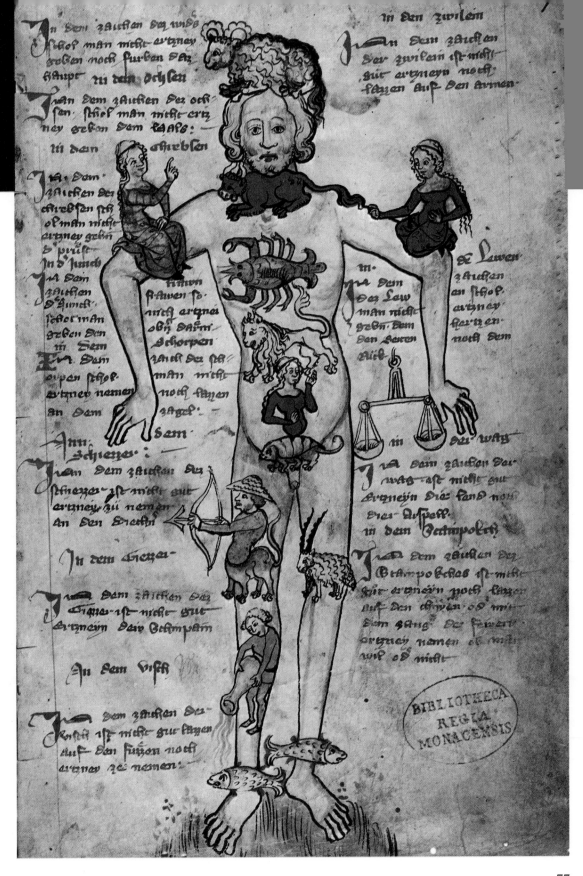

"Some amazingly accurate astrological forecasts"

burg who had been conscripted into the German army at the beginning of World War I.

The cause of his annoyance was simple enough—he had just finished a spell of guard duty and had been hoping to get some sleep. His puzzlement had a deeper source. He simply could not understand where his astrological calculations had gone wrong. For some months past Witte had kept a careful record of the occurrence of major Russian artillery barrages, and had checked them against the astrological conditions prevailing at the time. He had acquired such a knowledge of the planetary and zodiacal positions associated with previous Russian artillery assaults that he felt confident he could accurately predict the times and dates of future ones. But somehow an error had crept into his calculations. Witte had been sure that no barrage was due—but here he was, right in the middle of one.

Over the next few months he and a colleague who had worked with him on developing an astrological technique of bombardment forecasting puzzled over the matter. After much consideration and study the two men came to a surprising conclusion. They decided that there was another planet, unknown to either astronomers or astrologers, whose movements through the zodiac were throwing out their calculations. Witte called this hypothetical planet *Cupido*. He believed that it was situated beyond the orbit of Neptune. On the basis of the failures of his prediction technique, he worked out what he thought Cupido's movements were. Using these hypothetical movements in his horoscopes he claimed to be able to forecast artillery barrages with considerably greater—although not complete—accuracy.

In fact, at the time that Witte came to believe in the existence of Cupido there *was* an unknown planet beyond Neptune. It was not discovered until 1930, when it was named Pluto. The hypothetical orbit of Cupido was so different from that of Pluto, however, that Witte cannot be hailed as an astronomer ahead of his time. Nor is there the slightest evidence for the existence of seven further planets that Witte and his fellow astrologer Sieggrun claimed to discover beyond the orbit of Cupido. Nevertheless, Witte and Sieggrun worked out a detailed account of the movements of these alleged planets. They published these movements in tabular form, and they have resulted in some amazingly accurate astrological forecasts.

By the late 1920s the tables had become widely available. Astrologers who wished to do so could incorporate the positions of the so-called new planets of Cupido, Hades, Zeus, Chronos, Apollo, Admetos, Vulcan, and Poseidon in the horoscopes that they drew up. The few who chose to do so created the Hamburg School of astrology, as it was called.

Today the Hamburg School draws its supporters largely from Germany and Austria, but its adherents include one or two American and British astrologers. These astrologers calculate enormously complicated horoscopes with the aid of *The Rule Book for Planetary Pictures*—a textbook of Witte's system originally published in 1928—and a dial-like apparatus which all members of the School learn to operate.

Practitioners of the Hamburg School affirm that their system is capable of infallibly predicting the future, and of revealing

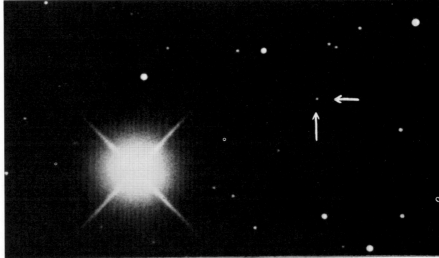

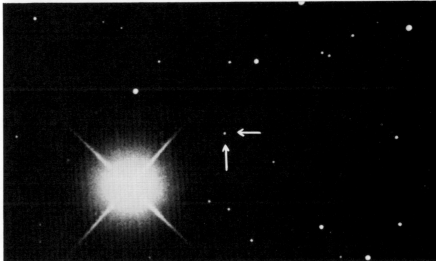

the exact nature of past events. Thus in the late 1950s Ludwig Stuiber, a Viennese engineer and a devotee of Witte's theories, published a series of short pamphlets entitled *Convincing Astrological Experiments*. These gave details of how Hamburg School techniques had been successfully used to answer even the most improbable questions. In one example Stuiber told how one Hamburg School astrologer had been given the time, date, and place of birth of a woman whose identity was completely unknown to him, and was asked, "What happened to this woman in Vienna at 4 p.m. on March 4, 1954?" After consulting his dial and rule book, the astrologer answered correctly: she had been shot in the back.

Herr Stuiber was a convinced believer in the theories of Alfred

Above: Reinhold Ebertin, the son of Elsbeth Ebertin who analyzed Hitler's horoscope with such spectacular accuracy. Her son considers himself an astrological pioneer, a "cosmobiologist." His astrological methods are decidedly antitraditional. He ignores such basic "normal" horoscope data as division into houses, and even pays little attention to the zodiac. However, his astrological texts are read with great interest by serious-minded astrologers not only in Germany but all over the world.

Witte and the Hamburg School, so it would be easy enough to believe that he had exaggerated or even invented stories of the system's infallibility. Curiously enough, however, astrologers who were skeptical of Witte's "new planets" and their use in astrology have sometimes found his system effective when they have lightheartedly experimented with it.

Odder still is the case of Ellic Howe, a distinguished historian of astrology. He does not believe in astrology himself, but he has learned to use its techniques in the course of his research. In his book *Urania's Children*, Howe tells how he was approached by Arthur Gauntlett, a professional British astrologer. Gauntlett challenged Howe to try to tell him what had happened to him on two specific days in the past. Although he expected nothing to come of his attempt, Howe applied Witte's system. To his own amazement he came up with answers which, according to Gauntlett, "were so extraordinarily close to the actual events that, had I not known otherwise, prior knowledge might have been suspected."

Such remarkable successes are perhaps coincidental, but the Hamburg School would seem to be worthy of further investigation. For although such planets as the hypothetical Cupido are almost certainly nonexistent, it is just possible—if extremely unlikely—that Witte had identified certain points in the solar system which, like the angles that form the aspects in a horoscope, have some unexplained astrological importance.

Whether or not this is so, the very existence of the Hamburg School is a reminder that, while we talk in general terms of "astrology" and "astrological methods," there are in reality a number of astrological systems. Most of these agree with one another except in points of detail, but some of them have almost completely abandoned the astrological traditions that have grown up over the centuries.

Apart from the members of the Hamburg School with their eight new planets, some of the most revolutionary modern astrologers are the German "cosmobiologists" associated with Reinhold Ebertin. Despite the success of his mother Elsbeth Ebertin—who always used traditional methods and who forecast Hitler's future with such accuracy—Reinhold Ebertin has thrown overboard what he calls "astrology's medieval ballast." He and his fellow cosmobiologists concentrate on complexes of planets situated on a common axis. They pay little attention to the signs of the zodiac.

The overwhelming majority of Western astrologers, however, do not believe that it is necessary or desirable to go so far. They admit that there are some out-of-date elements in their tradition, some absurd superstitions, and a few crude suppositions, but they feel that the traditional system is basically sound. They hold that the use of the zodiac is a key—perhaps *the* key—to astrology.

The zodiac is a circular band of sky extending about eight degrees on either side of the *ecliptic*—the apparent path of the Sun through the sky. The zodiac band is called the "racetrack of the planets." As we look into the heavens from Earth, we see the planets always within this belt of sky. Although the Earth and the other planets revolve around the Sun, from Earth it appears that the Sun, Moon, and planets are moving around the

Earth, tracking their circular pathway within the zodiac band.

As almost everyone knows, there are 12 signs of the zodiac: Aries, Taurus, Gemini, Cancer, Leo, Virgo, Libra, Scorpio, Saggitarius, Capricorn, Aquarius, and Pisces. It was the Babylonians who first divided the zodiac into 12. They noticed that the zodiac contained 12 major constellations, and they named each section of the zodiac after the constellation that lay within it.

However, the 12 signs of the zodiac as we know them today no longer correspond with the constellations that bear the same names. For example, if you were born between September 24 and October 23, it is said that your Sun Sign is Libra—meaning that the Sun was in that particular sign on the date of your birth. (During the year the Sun takes to pass through the zodiac, it appears to stay in each sign for 30 days.) Today this does not mean that you were born under the *group of stars* called Libra, however. That might have been true two or three thousand years ago, when the Sun did appear to be among the Libra group of stars during that period of the year. But today the constellation of Libra is many degrees away from the sign of the same name. This is because the Earth's axis has a slight wobble, and the zones of the zodiac as we see them from Earth are no longer in line with the constellations that gave them their names. This slow shift in the sky pattern as we on Earth view it takes 25,800 years to come full circle. At the end of that period, therefore, the constellations and the signs once more coincide; but they immediately start to diverge again.

Modern astrologers are not concerned with the constellations as such, but only with the signs. They divide the zodiac circle of 360° into 12 equal and precisely defined zones of 30°, each

KOSMOBIOLOGIE

Mitteilungsblatt des „Arbeitskreises für kosmobiologische Forschung" und der „Kosmobiologischen Akademie Aalen, Arbeitsgemeinschaft e. V."

MENSCH IM ALL

30. Jahrgang   1   Januar 1963

AUS DEM INHALT:

Zum Beginn des 30. Jahrgangs

Möglichkeiten und Grenzen kosmischer Thematik

Die persönlichen Punkte im Kosmogramm

Médium coeli = Ichbewußtsein

Abnormitäten

u. a.

Left: Ebertin's *Kosmobiologie*, the most reputable German magazine devoted to astrology. Reinhold Ebertin founded it originally in 1928, and then resumed publication after World War II in Aalen, where he has now also established an annual astrological conference.

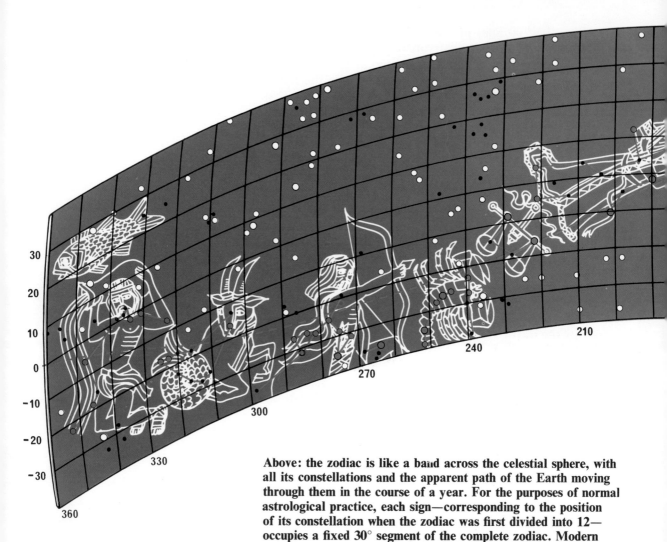

30

20

10

0

−10

−20

−30

360

330

300

270

240

210

Above: the zodiac is like a band across the celestial sphere, with all its constellations and the apparent path of the Earth moving through them in the course of a year. For the purposes of normal astrological practice, each sign—corresponding to the position of its constellation when the zodiac was first divided into 12— occupies a fixed 30° segment of the complete zodiac. Modern astrologers work only with the signs, not the constellations.

Below: the zodiac is a symbolic concept rather than an astronomical entity, but if it did appear in the heavens, it would circle the Earth like this, lying inside the huge sphere of the heavens, imagined as enclosing our world.

represented by a sign. The signs are therefore fixed. The Sun is always in Libra for the period September 24 to October 23, just as it is always in Scorpio for the period October 24 to November 22, and so on.

Almost all of us know our Sun Sign, and we have probably read at least one account of the characteristics attached to it. These portraits of character and abilities can be remarkably accurate if we happen to be a pure zodiacal type—a person whose horoscope is heavily influenced by one particular sign. If your Sun Sign is Capricorn, for example, and you happen to have been born at sunrise, Capricorn would also be your *ascendant*— the sign that was rising above the eastern horizon at the time of your birth. This would reinforce the effect of your Sun Sign. If Saturn, Capricorn's ruling planet, were present in the sign at the moment when you were born, this would also enhance your Capricornian characteristics. Again, your horoscope might contain several planets at significant angles in the sign of Capricorn. These would also help to make you a "typical Capricornian."

However, few of us possess such a straightforward astrological makeup. We are not one in 12, but one in a million! Even though

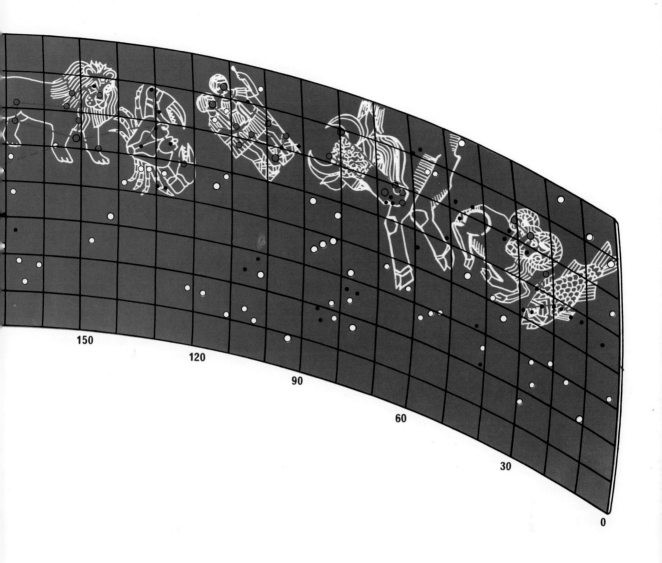

you were born when the Sun was in Capricorn, for instance, you
might have had another sign in the ascendant at birth. Similarly
you might have several planets in Leo or Pisces or Aquarius, and
these will greatly modify the typically Capricornian characteristics in your nature. In certain circumstances in fact, you may
be far more like another Sun Sign character than a Capricornian.

Nevertheless the Sun Signs are important, and you will probably
recognize some aspects of your character in the description of
your own Sun Sign. But you need not reject astrology because
these portraits do not fit your personality completely if you bear
in mind how other signs may have been present and influential
in your horoscope. You are in any case likely to find that some
of the statements concerning your Sun Sign are generally accurate, and a few may pinpoint your personality to perfection.
Some will doubtlessly be inaccurate.

One other point must be made about the following material on
Sun Signs. Because pure zodiacal types are so rare, the people
listed as examples have been chosen as being *of the character* of
each Sun Sign. They may in some cases have been born under a
different Sun Sign, of which they are less typical.

Aries

ARIES *the Ram* (March 21 to April 20)

Early in the last century the astrologer Raphael described the typical Aries person as "commanding, choleric, and violent." Modern astrologers use politer language, but in essence their opinion is basically the same. Aries people are seen as adventurous, pioneering types, respected but not always loved for their independence, their reliance on facts rather than feelings or theories, and their happy concentration upon themselves. This self-absorption is, strangely enough, usually free from any taint of vanity.

Aries is traditionally the most masculine of the signs, and the Aries man tends to have all the characteristics of the "male chauvinist." He takes his own virility for granted—although he sometimes has difficulty in recognizing this quality in other men. Where sex is concerned, he sees himself as a conqueror. The Aries woman also has many qualities still sometimes regarded as typically masculine. She tends to be boisterous and to take the lead in a relationship if she can do so. Ideally, she needs a partner as strong as herself.

The Aries desire for competition and independence makes success at work important to people born under this sign. They want to get to the top of their chosen field. And they may choose careers like gardening, sculpture, public relations, and sport—anything that combines plenty of energetic activity with some, but not too much, theory.

Some examples of people with strong Aries characteristics are show business personalities Louis Armstrong, Marlon Brando, Bette Davis, and Charlie Chaplin; political leader Nikita Krushchev; painter Vincent Van Gogh; novelists George Sand and Emile Zola; and conductors Leopold Stokowski and Arturo Toscanini.

Vincent van Gogh

Right: the pushy independence of Aries shows itself in the work of the painter Van Gogh, whose paintings were so far in advance of current artistic taste that it has taken critics decades to appreciate his original genius. His impetuosity is recorded in his reckless gesture of remorse in which he cut off his own ear.

Charlie Chaplin

Right: Chaplin, shown in a still with child star Jackie Coogan from his first full-length feature *The Kid*, shows his typically Arian character in his determined and ambitious drive, which brought him out of a poverty-stricken childhood to a position of unique eminence in the history of the development of motion pictures.

Right: astrologers in the past considered that Arians might even look like the Ram of their sign. The pictures of Jefferson and Van Gogh shown below do bear a certain resemblance to this Arian type.

Thomas Jefferson

Below: a man of wide and deep intellectual interests, Jefferson had an enterprising and practical turn of mind which is often a characteristic of the Aries sign.

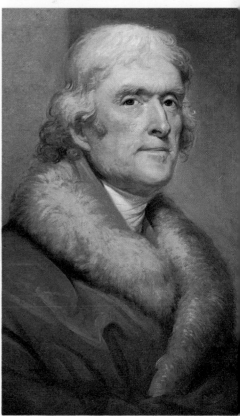

Taurus

TAURUS *the Bull* (April 21 to May 21)

Taurus is an earthy sign, and pure Taureans tend to be slow but sure, like the measured tread of the bull that gives the sign its name. Some astrologers of the past even went so far as to suggest that Taureans look like bulls—thick-necked, thickset, and wide of nostrils. Taurus people have a taste for the good things of life, enjoying both work and leisure to the full and taking pleasure in food, drink, material possessions, and affection.

The Taurus man combines self-centeredness with generosity, and is capable of becoming an ideal husband and father. He generally has a friendly attitude toward other men and is slow to respond to provocation. When he does become angry, however, others must beware. Like the bull, his reactions are slow—but he is terrible in his rage. The Taurus woman is strong-minded but does not impose her views on others. She makes a true friend, a perfect wife, and an ideal mother, never trying to dominate her husband or her children.

Where work is concerned, Taureans tend to be competent in most fields, but they are particularly good at jobs pertaining to money and to the earth that marks their sign. They shine as bankers, cashiers, geologists, or potters, and they usually like a job with plenty of security. Famous Taureans and Taurean types include George Washington, Karl Marx, Sigmund Freud, William Shakespeare, Johannes Brahms, Margot Fonteyn, Fred Astaire, Bing Crosby, Gary Cooper, Orson Welles, Honoré de Balzac, and Arnold Bennett.

Karl Marx

Left: Marx showed his Taurean traits in his strong determination and in his husbandly devotion to his faithful wife. He appeared to contemporaries mainly as a coldly arrogant man, full of hate—a reflection of the negative Taurean trait of slow but terrible rage.

Left: astrological physiognomists thought the typical Taurean would look like a bull—thickset, thick-necked, with a broad forehead.

Below: Taurus, from a 10th-century Indian horoscope. Notice that this Taurean bull is the humped bull, still the bull of India today.

Ulysses S. Grant

Left: Grant's relentlessness, so typical of the Taurean, led him to conceive tactics that crushed Confederate resistance, but also meant that in his stubbornness he refused to give up his corrupt presidential advisors and refused to—or was unable to—recognize their callous misuse of his trust.

Honoré de Balzac

Right: the earthy character of Taurus as exemplified not only in Balzac's personality, but even in his solid, bull-like appearance.

Gemini

GEMINI *the Twins* (May 22 to June 21)

The pure Gemini is born under a double sign and is a dual personality, forever shifting his or her outlook on life. Gemini is the patron sign of intellectuals, egocentrics, and the mentally unstable. Gemini people tend to be fickle and to change their opinions constantly to suit themselves. They also enjoy arguing, and their conversation is full of twists and turns.

The duality of the sign is typified by the Gemini man. He can talk himself into love with great speed—and out again just as quickly. He has an easy charm and a captivating manner, but tends to be unreliable and even downright disloyal. The Gemini woman has similar characteristics, although her restlessness and changeability are often muted by the pressures exerted upon her by society.

Gemini people hate monotonous work. They need jobs that will give full scope to their agility and urge for change. The factory production line is not for them, but they excel at any kind of work that involves movement and variety—lecturing, publishing, and almost any kind of craftsmanship.

Some well-known Geminis and Gemini personalities are political leader John F. Kennedy; the Duke of Edinburgh; the composer Richard Wagner; the painter Paul Gauguin; Conan Doyle, author of the Sherlock Holmes stories, and Ian Fleming, the creator of James Bond; playwright George Bernard Shaw; movie stars Marilyn Monroe, Judy Garland, and Errol Flynn; and song writer Bob Dylan.

Paul Gauguin

Right: one of Gauguin's paintings. The restless Gemini urge for change and travel led Gauguin to abandon his family and cross the world to Tahiti, where he painted his savagely splendid masterpieces.

Marilyn Monroe

Below right: the sensitive and highly strung Gemini is typified in the troubled, restless life of the famous blonde sex symbol, who died of an overdose of drugs.

Left: even cities can have their sign, and London's is Gemini. With this drawing of the Gemini twins tumbling into the fire, the 17th-century astrologer William Lilly foretold the Fire of London.

Queen Victoria

Right: her ascendant was Gemini, and although in many ways she was untypical, her letters show the Geminian flair for lively writing.

Cancer

CANCER *the Crab* (June 22 to July 22)

Despite the tough-looking crab that gives this sign its name, Cancerians are motherly gentle people. Like the crab, however, pure Cancerians tend to appear all hardness on the outside, while inside their shells they are soft, vulnerable, and easily hurt. Beneath the mask of a tough and ultralogical personality, they are extremely moody and emotional. They are, like the crab, deeply attached to their homes. This is unquestionably the sign of the man or woman whose home life is the keynote of his or her existence. A Cancerian can be a social asset, and knows a great deal about good food and wine.

The Cancer man is likely to have had an especially close relationship with his mother, and the effects of this usually last into adult life. He tends to keep his emotional distance from other human beings, and may try to cast his partner in a mother role, at least some of the time.

Cancer women tend to be gentle home-loving wives who find the raising of children their most rewarding occupation. They are attracted to two types of men: the weak, well-intentioned male who appeals to their motherly feelings, and the hard, almost brutal type who dominates them and exploits their gentleness. The best partner for a Cancer woman is usually an equally home-centered man.

Cancerians are good at any job in which they do not have to dominate. They are made for occupations connected with the home or children, and for handling people who are going through a difficult time. They therefore make splendid physicians, nurses, and social workers.

Among Cancerians and Cancer types are the painters Rembrandt, Salvador Dali, and Marc Chagall; the philosopher Jean-Jacques Rousseau; the composer Franz Schubert; the poet Lord Byron; writers Jean Cocteau and Marcel Proust; movie director Ingmar Bergman; and actress Gina Lollobrigida.

Marcel Proust

Above: typically Cancerian in his attachment to his mother, Proust retreated to his famous cork-lined study when she died and buried himself in his writing, producing his intricately woven masterpiece.

90

Salvador Dali

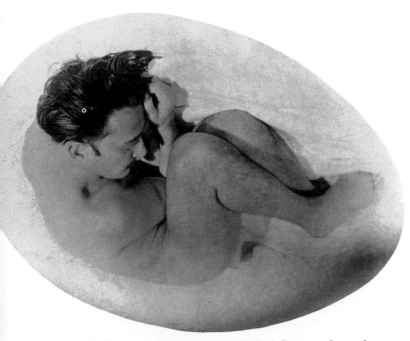

Left: this representation of Dali as a fetus in an egg ties up with the Cancerian link with birth and fertility. Dali is a clear example of Cancerian sensitivity, Cancer being his ascendant.

Below: a symbolic representation of the United States, whose sign is Cancer from its "birthday" of July 4, 1776. A strong paternal instinct has shaped recent world history. Detractors might also call it Cancerian in its oversensitivity to criticism.

John Glenn

Above: the first astronaut to circle the world, Glenn is a Cancer type in his tenacity of purpose that sustained him through the rigors of the space training program. His excellent memory is another typical characteristic of Cancer.

Leo

LEO *the Lion* (July 23 to August 23)

Leos are extroverts—men and women with a strong presence, a vital magnetism, and an urge to dominate. They like to be in the spotlight, not hovering at the back of the stage.

Leo men are confident of their abilities and their sex appeal, and women tend either to love or loathe a Leo man. At his best the Leo man is a splendid leader; at his worst he is a vain bullying bore.

Leo women are also self-assured, and often want to dominate their partners. They love to be pampered and to lead a life of luxury. They tend to be impractical, preferring a mink coat to a dishwasher, a diamond ring to a typewriter.

Leos do well in any occupation that enables them to dominate others or to be the center of attention. Thus careers in politics, theatre, organizing, or lecturing attract them most strongly, and suit them best.

Notable Leos and Leo types include the political leaders Benito Mussolini, Fidel Castro, and Bismarck; the rulers Louis XIV (the Sun King) of France and the Emperor Napoleon; the painters Rubens and Picasso; the psychologist Carl Jung; the poet Robert Burns; writers Aldous Huxley and John Galsworthy; the movie director Alfred Hitchcock; and the public figure Jacqueline Kennedy Onassis.

Napoleon Bonaparte

Right: a typical Leo, Napoleon had unquestioning assurance that he was the person who knew best how the world should be organized, and mobilized his own considerable talents—and those of France—to make sure he was in a position to arrange matters to his satisfaction. He could be magnanimous, but he was ruthless to those who tried to challenge his Leonine command.

Orville Wright

Below: for him the creativity of a Leo type was expressed in the long struggle to design a craft that would actually fly. This picture shows him at the controls, lifting into the first flight.

Benito Mussolini

Left: the Italian dictator was a Leo from the beginning in his unusually pugnacious and self-assertive qualities when in his first school year. He had the Leonine gift for breadth of vision, but with it a flamboyant braggadocio. This picture of him with his chin thrust forward shows one of his favorite public stances.

Otto, Prince von Bismarck

Above: a Leo type, the militaristic Bismarck had a vision of a grand design, but impatience with the details. Typically, he clung too long to power, and was at last dismissed to bitter retirement.

Virgo

VIRGO *the Virgin*
(August 24 to September 23)

Virgos combine intelligence and common sense. They are neat, tidy, conscious of the need for order, likely to hoard things, and sometimes almost obsessed with the need for cleanliness.

Their belief in order and doing it right sometimes makes Virgo men seem like human calculating machines. Their precision and neatness does not fit into the conventional image of masculinity. They are rarely capable of really letting go, and even their sex lives may be distinguished for technique rather than enthusiasm.

Virgo women cannot be satisfied with merely exploiting their feminine charms. They want to perform a task in life, and to perform it well. They infinitely prefer honest recognition of their material achievements to idle flattery. They want a partner who lives up to their own high standards. Once they get him they will give him all the supportive love he needs.

Virgos dislike unskilled work, but enjoy any kind of job that requires them to impose order on chaos. They are outstanding in fields that give their neatness and desire for perfection full play. Scientific research, accountancy, record maintenance, or secretarial work are made for Virgos.

Virgo people and types include the statesman Cardinal Richelieu, Prince Albert, the husband of Queen Victoria, former President Lyndon Johnson, the writers Leo Tolstoy, Goethe, and D. H. Lawrence, and movie stars Greta Garbo, Lauren Bacall, Sophia Loren, and Peter Sellers.

Leo Tolstoy

Left: Tolstoy possessed fully the Virgoan zest for work, and his ruthless analytical powers are a vivid example of the Virgo type. In his quest for perfection, he typically lost sight of the forest for the trees, and the sad end of his marriage and family life are a bleak testimonial to his unrelenting struggle to find a morally good pattern of life.

Right: Virgo the maiden, from an 18-century celestial atlas. Traditionally Virgo is represented with a sheaf of corn in her hand. This ties in with the time of harvest when the sign occurs.

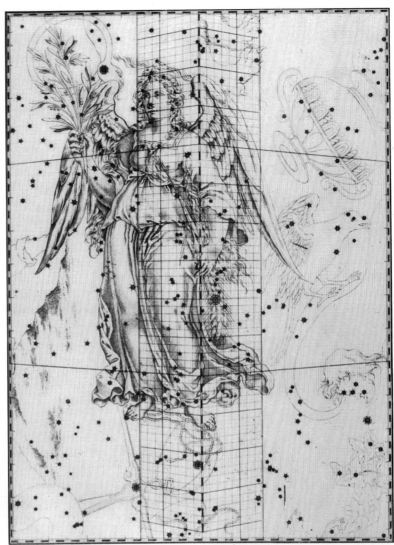

Johann Wolfgang von Goethe

Left: the Virgoan gift for natural philosophy shows brilliantly in Goethe's masterpieces of poetry and drama, and his genius for intellectual discrimination was another typical Virgoan trait.

Louis XIV

Right: though the planets' positions in his horoscope would tend to make the Sun King a Leo type, his passion for perfection shows that he was indeed born under Virgo.

95

Libra

LIBRA *the Scales*
(September 24 to October 23)

Pure Librans are the salt of the earth. They want to be liked and to like others. Their gentle, tolerant, and diplomatic natures make it perfectly easy for others to get along with them. The scales are their sign, and they tend to be balanced individuals with moderate views who are repelled by extremism of any kind. The Libran's chief failing is being too easily influenced.

The Libra man is in no way effeminate, but to other men he sometimes appears so. This need not worry the Libran—there is nothing to be ashamed of in being sociable, courteous, and cultured. A Libra man is usually attractive to women, although they may dislike his tendency to be so moderate that he never puts forward an independent point of view.

Libra is the most feminine of the signs, and Libra women are exceptionally feminine. In love they display charm and gentleness—as they do to some extent in all their personal relationships—but they know how to use these qualities for their own ends. They get a great deal of happiness from a satisfactory home life and enjoy the company of their children.

Librans tend to be lazy rather than industrious, and jobs that involve strenuous physical effort have little appeal for them. They do well in almost any occupation connected with art, legal matters, diplomacy, and dealing with other people.

Characteristic Libra personalities and Librans include Erasmus, the great 16th-century scholar and humanist; Mahatma Gandhi, the political and religious leader and apostle of nonviolence; the painter Watteau; the composer Franz Liszt; occultist Aleister Crowley; the poet T. S. Eliot; writers Oscar Wilde, Graham Greene, William Faulkner, and Katherine Mansfield; and actresses Sarah Bernhardt and Brigitte Bardot.

Above: Botticelli's enduring *The Birth of Venus*. Venus is the ruling planet of Libra, the most feminine of the zodiacal signs, and it is the rulership of Venus that makes those born under Libra typically charming, artistic, and refined. The influence of Venus in Libra is strongly toward goodness and happiness, and the typical Libran is likeable and even-tempered, if a little lazy.

Brigitte Bardot

Left: easy-going, charming, and liking harmony, BB is a typical Libran in her relaxed attitude toward life— but must guard against the equally typical Libran indecision.

Oscar Wilde

Above: Libran sociability, culture, and wit were well exemplified in Wilde's career. Perhaps in the tragic end it also showed the Libran danger of recklessness.

Scorpio

SCORPIO *the Scorpion*
(October 24 to November 22)

In the past this sign had a sinister reputation, being associated with death, decay, and deceit. Scorpio people have even been said to have the look of scorpions and snakes.

Since the 17th century, however, such dark views of Scorpio have become less and less fashionable, and present-day astrologers concentrate on the positive aspects of the sign. Only a minority of Scorpio people, they say, reflect the more sinister side of the sign. Most Scorpios are reasonable, life-loving, and honest people. They are often difficult to get along with, however, because of their secretiveness, their fierce will power, and their strong likes and dislikes.

The Scorpio man is intensely conscious of his self-integrity, and displays a keen sense of personal pride. His outstanding characteristics are his aggressiveness and his eroticism. He takes a long time to make up his mind about whether he loves someone, but once he has committed himself he rarely changes course. However, on the rare occasions when he does change his mind about his love life, his beliefs, or his choice of career, he does so abruptly and violently. The Scorpio man doesn't set out to please, but is usually good company.

The Scorpio woman has all the characteristics of her male counterpart although she usually displays them less aggressively. She has a strong and mysterious sex appeal even when she is not physically attractive. She is tenacious in love, and is driven by an urge for power, sexual and otherwise.

Scorpio people like hard work as much as Librans loathe it. They have a serious attitude toward most aspects of life, and have even been said to "make work of their play." Their extreme competitiveness combined with their authoritarianism often brings them success in a military career or other occupation in which they can give the orders. Any tough and demanding job—mining, electronics, working on an oil rig—will attract Scorpio people, and they excel as police detectives, security guards, attorneys, and surgeons.

Famous Scorpios and those like Scorpios include the prime minister Indira Gandhi; military leader and dictator General Franco; general and statesman Charles de Gaulle; Kemal Ataturk, the brilliant soldier who created modern Turkey; Horatio Nelson, the British admiral who won the Battle of Trafalgar; Mata Hari, the World War I spy and *femme fatale*; Marie Curie, the co-discoverer of radium; writers Victor Hugo, Dostoyevsky, Goethe, and Edgar Allan Poe; singer Edith Piaf; and, illustrating the darker side of the sign, Hitler's lieutenants Herman Göring and Joseph Goebbels.

Marie Curie

Above: the strong determination that is associated with this sign was clearly obvious in the life of Madame Curie, pictured with her husband Pierre, with whom she discovered radium. She fully demonstrates the Scorpian passion for hard work. In fact, the type excels in careers requiring close and detailed research work.

98

Pablo Picasso

Below: perhaps the most characteristic trait of the true Scorpian is intensity, as can be seen in Picasso's *Weeping Woman*. In his life, he showed other typical Scorpian tendencies of jealousy, ruthlessness, and—most obviously—wholly original creativity.

Mata Hari

Left: one of the definite Scorpian traits is eroticism. Since the sign rules hidden things, it is perhaps not unexpected that the Dutch girl with Scorpio as her Sun Sign became a German spy, built on a career of amorous and political intrigue which ended at last with her execution.

Theodore Roosevelt

Right: the forceful personality and varied interests of Roosevelt (left) are typical of the positive side of Scorpio. Ted Roosevelt was also Scorpian in his ambition and decisiveness, which made him a natural leader and a popular president. Sickly as a child, in his adult life he welcomed all opportunities to test his strength.

Sagittarius

SAGITTARIUS *the Archer*
(November 23 to December 21)

Sagittarius is a sign particularly associated with success, and fate usually gives the Sagittarian more than one opportunity to achieve it. However, Sagittarians tend to be so happy-go-lucky that they often fail to seize the chances that are offered to them. At best, Sagittarians are highly talented individuals who are interested in almost everything. At worst, they waste their talents in too many fields and become pathetic braggarts.

The Sagittarian man has an outspoken and generous approach to life, and yet somehow other men tend to pick quarrels with him. He is lovable, but often resists the love that is offered for fear of losing his freedom. He loves animals, yet cannot resist the pleasure of hunting.

The Sagittarian woman shares these paradoxical qualities. She prefers activities outside the home to what she sees as the dull round of the housewife. Nevertheless, she makes a good mother, and never a possessive one.

Sagittarians have a genius for communication, and they will succeed at any skilled task in the fields of journalism, television, advertising, publishing, or consultancy work. Where less skilled jobs are concerned, they are prepared to tackle anything that leaves them a certain amount of freedom.

Sagittarian types and Sagittarians include Abraham Lincoln, Winston Churchill, Beethoven, the poet John Milton, writers Mark Twain, Noel Coward, and John Osborne, humorist James Thurber, singers Maria Callas, Frank Sinatra, and Sammy Davies, and moviemaker Walt Disney.

Walt Disney

Right: in his creation of Mickey Mouse and many other cartoon characters that seem to have life and personality, Disney expressed the Sagittarian love of animals.

Below: the star map of Sagittarius, half man and half animal—the centaur with his bow drawn. Many Sagittarians are keen horsemen.

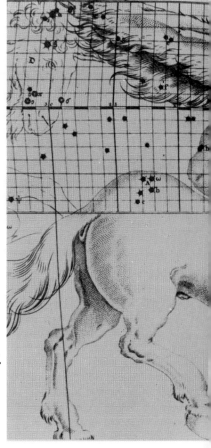

Ludwig von Beethoven

Sagittarian expansiveness and magnificence is typified by the music of Beethoven—grand, full, echoing down the centuries with overwhelming vitality. Equally typical determination is shown in his life and his dogged persistence in composing after he became deaf.

William Blake

Right: Blake's painting of Isaac Newton. In his passion for meeting the challenge of a problem—often technical difficulties he found in painting or engraving—Blake was typical of less-often recognized but strongly Sagittarian traits.

© Walt Disney Productions, 1976

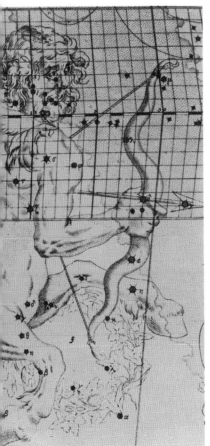

Sir Winston Churchill

Right: blunt, dogged, resolved to meet problems head on, Churchill was a true Sagittarian. Also like others of his Sun Sign, Churchill had a great gift of communication.

James Thurber

Below: the Sagittarian love of animals expresses itself in the dogs that Thurber drew so often —and the real ones which he and his wife raised as dog breeders.

Capricorn

CAPRICORN *the Goat*
(December 22 to January 20)

"One does not invite to dinner the same evening Leo and Capricorn," wrote astrologer Rupert Gleadow. This was probably good advice, for the characteristics of the two signs are almost directly opposite. As the Leo is outgoing, dominating, and attention seeking, the Capricorn is introverted, submissive, and self-effacing. Yet Capricorn people are extremely ambitious, and burn with a desire to succeed. They do not usually seek success in a dramatic way, however. The Capricorn person goes in for long, painstaking struggles whose real nature others ignore, but which eventually take him or her to the top.

Capricorn men tend to have a traditional and unbending approach toward women—a rigidity that both attracts and repels. They are intensely competitive in their attitudes toward other men, and usually command respect rather than affection.

The Capricorn woman likes to be in a position of power, whether within her own family or in the outside world. She is loyal and astute, and often possesses a rather hard veneer of glamour. She is affectionate to her husband and children, but is never really happy if her life is confined to the home, for at heart she always remains a career woman.

Capricorn people are good at most occupations that do not require a high degree of imagination. They excel at monotonous tasks, whether clerical or physical. Their passion for detail and exactness makes them good teachers of subjects like mathematics or science, where there is a definite answer to most questions. In the arts they are usually imitators rather than originators. They can rise to the top of any profession in which effort, accuracy, and determination are the key qualities for success.

Famous Capricornians and those much like them include Woodrow Wilson, Stalin, the philosopher Kant, scientists Johannes Kepler, Isaac Newton, and Louis Pasteur, the missionary Albert Schweitzer, cellist Pablo Casals, beauty expert Helena Rubinstein, and millionaire Howard Hughes.

Henri Matisse

Right: the deep love of beauty of Capricorns showed itself in the prolific work of this artist, also typical in his independent approach.

Sir Isaac Newton

Below: a portrait of Newton. He was Capricornian in his accuracy, determination, and self-reliance. This led him to revolutionize the course of scientific thought.

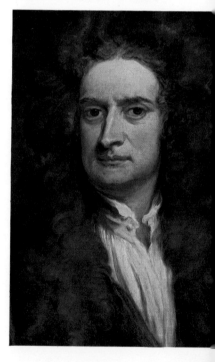

Josef Stalin

Above: Capricornians are often drawn to politics, and Stalin showed the dark side of the sign in his ruthless use of power.

Benjamin Franklin

Left: Franklin demonstrates the dry subtle Capricornian sense of humor in his writings and talk.

103

Aquarius

AQUARIUS *the Water Carrier*
(January 21 to February 19)

The highest aim of the typical Aquarian is personal freedom. Unlike the Capricornian, the Aquarian has little respect for convention or tradition if it obstructs the liberty of the individual. Aquarians are humanitarians, and the freedom of others is almost as important to them as their own. They tend to take an intellectual approach to life, but this never makes them cold or unemotional, and they are often active in groups formed for a social cause—political reform, or the protection of the environment, for example. They are open-minded, and willing to listen to the other person's point of view, although they also have a reputation for being tactless and sometimes obstinate.

The Aquarian man is free of vanity, yet intensely conscious of his dignity as a human being. He despises traditionally masculine values and is the very opposite of a "male chauvinist," treating women as fellow human beings and not mere sexual objects.

Aquarian women are also strong believers in sexual equality, and today are often active members of Women's Liberation. They have an adventurous approach to life. They hate to be dominated sexually or financially, and are at their best with partners who share their belief in the importance of the individual.

For Aquarians work is not primarily a way of making money but a vocation in which their love of freedom can find expression. They are at their best when self-employed or engaged in work that involves helping others, such as medicine, psychology, social work, or politics.

Aquarians and Aquarian personalities include political leader Franklin D. Roosevelt; the 16th-century astronomer Galileo; the naturalist Charles Darwin who formulated the theory of evolution; the aviator Charles Lindbergh; the essayist and philosopher Francis Bacon; writers Charles Dickens, Lewis Carroll, and Somerset Maugham; actresses Vanessa Redgrave and Jeanne Moreau; and actor Paul Newman.

Charles Lindbergh

Above: Aquarian originality and genius for inventiveness, often expressed in scientific work, is clear in Lindbergh's character —as was his love of adventure.

Wolfgang Amadeus Mozart

Left: Aquarians are often clever children, and Mozart's career as a child prodigy is well known. As an adult, however, he was untypical in his use of conventional musical forms, apparently feeling little need to try experiments.

James Dean

Below: his sensitive good looks were typically Aquarian—as was the youthful spirit of rebellion against convention, which he came to typify during his career.

Pisces

PISCES *the Fishes*
(February 20 to March 20)

At their best Pisceans are idealists. At their worst they are dropouts and hoboes. They are amiable, vague, and sometimes devious. They have an easy attitude to life, and are liable to be too easily influenced by others. They are the very opposite of egotistical—some of them seem hardly conscious that they have an ego—and they tend to oppose material values with what they consider to be spiritual ones. Pisceans are lovable people because they themselves are very loving.

The Pisces man is rarely effeminate, but he tends to display unashamedly the feminine components of the personality that most men are anxious to conceal. To some women he appears too soft and gentle, but to others his easy-going ways are attractive. He is little suited to the harsh rough and tumble of a purely masculine environment, but he feels thoroughly at home in artistic circles.

The Pisces woman is many men's idea of the perfect partner—loving, tender, submissive, and anxious to please. At the same time, no Piscean wants to be bullied, and she will avoid this by guile rather than outright opposition.

Pisceans are not naturally hard workers, for they lack the motivations of ambition or love of money. Some Pisceans, however, have a passionate desire to serve their fellow human beings, and they can work hard for a cause in spite of their lack of dynamism. On the whole Pisceans do best in jobs connected, however vaguely, with the arts—from doorman at a gallery or concert hall to painter or musician.

Outstanding Piscean types and Pisceans include the ballet dancers Vaslav Nijinsky and Rudolf Nureyev; the poet Hölderlin and the poetess Elizabeth Browning; the composers Handel, Chopin, and Rimsky Korsakov; the opera singer Enrico Caruso; artists Michelangelo and Auguste Renoir; playwright Edward Albee; novelist John Steinbeck; and actress Elizabeth Taylor.

Pisces joins with Aries to complete the zodiac circle. Whether the portrait of your Sun Sign fits you well or not, it is a good idea to take a look at all the signs. That way you may gain an inkling of the other sign, or signs, that might play an important role in your horoscope. For even two people born on the same day, and perhaps only a few minutes apart, can have very different horoscopes. The way to find out the signs that count in your life is to draw up your own personal star chart—and that is not as hard as it sounds.

Vaslav Nijinsky

Above: Piscean instability and hypersensitivity are obvious in the tragic life of the legendary dancer. Only 10 years after his meteoric success, he left ballet to spend the last 30 years of his life in a mental hospital.

Frédéric Chopin

Right: some of the greatest artists —those who have been able to use their emotions through their work—have been Piscean, and in Chopin's case, the melancholy sensitivity was turned into his exquisite and subtle music.

106

Buonarotti Michelangelo

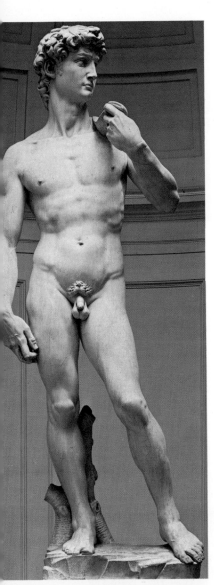

Left: Michelangelo was another Piscean, and like others under his sign, did not take kindly to outside attempts at regimentation.

Elizabeth Taylor

Below: some astrologers say that Pisces is such a receptive sign that it picks up infection quickly, and certainly this star's career has been marked by spectacular illnesses of a serious nature.

Your Personal Star Chart

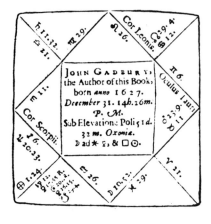

Identifying your Sun Sign may tell you something about yourself, but to read your stars you need to have a fuller picture of the position of the zodiac at the time and place of your birth. Above: a 17th-century horoscope of the astrologer John Gadbury drawn up in the old square style, which continued to be used long after it was generally accepted that the world was not flat. Right: the more familiar circular horoscope used in modern astrology.

Astrologers are the first to emphasize that judgments based purely on a person's Sun Sign can be wildly inaccurate and misleading. Yet few of us have any other basis on which to form an opinion of astrology's validity. We may not be willing, or able, to pay a highly qualified astrologer for a detailed horoscope. Nor may we want to spend many hours poring over books several times the length of this one to learn the basic techniques of constructing and interpreting a horoscope.

It is possible, however, to draw up and interpret your own personal map of the zodiac in a few simple stages. This chart is

"The heavens at the time and place of your birth"

not a detailed horoscope, but it will tell you a great deal more about astrology—and about yourself—than a simple Sun Sign description. Its interpretation will not, of course, be as full or as satisfactory as the one derived from a complete horoscope. But it should prove interesting and self-revealing, and it will probably help you to decide whether to go still further with the study of astrology.

The star chart is your personal map of the zodiac—a picture of the heavens as they appeared at the time and place of your birth. The first step in making the chart is to calculate your time of birth in Star Time. Star Time—usually known as *sidereal time*—is measured by the stars and not, like clock time, by the Sun. To every 24 hours of clock time there are 24 hours 2 minutes and $56\frac{1}{2}$ seconds of Star Time.

Anyone who can add or subtract can calculate the time of their birth in Star Time, and there is a simple formula to help you make this calculation with ease.

The formula is $S + T + A + $ or $ - R$.

S stands for Star Time at midnight on the day of birth. A list of the Star Times to the nearest minute at midnight on every day of the year from 1900 to 1975 is given in Tables 1 and 2 opposite.

Supposing you were born on January 10, 1934. You will see from the list of years printed at the foot of Table 1 that for 1934 you have to add one minute to the figure found opposite the date January 10 in the table. The time given for January 10 is 7:14. To this you add one minute, which gives you 7:15. This is the figure for the S in your formula, which now reads:

7 hrs. 15 mins. $+ T + A + $ or $ - R$

T stands for the local time of your birth. That means the ordinary clock time used where you were born—Eastern Standard Time in New York, for example, or Greenwich Mean Time in Britain. If you were born in the summer and the place of your birth was on daylight savings time in the year when you were born, you will have to deduct one hour from the clock time of your birth. You can usually get information on daylight savings time at your local library. If you were one of the small minority born in Britain during the recent period of Double British Summer Time the deduction will be two hours.

Let us take an example, saying that you were born in New York at 6 a.m. Eastern Standard Time. Because we have taken your date of birth to be January 10—right in the middle of winter—there is no need to make any adjustment for daylight or summer time, and your T figure is simply 6 hours 0 minutes. If your time of birth had been six in the *evening*, the T figure would have been 18 hours 0 minutes because astrology uses a 24-hour clock.

Your personal formula now reads:

7 hrs. 15 mins. $+ 6$ hrs. 0 mins. $+ A + $ or $ - R$

The A of our formula stand for "acceleration"—the adjustment for the difference in length between the clock day and the star day. This is roughly 10 seconds for each hour between midnight and the time of birth. We assumed your time of birth was 6 a.m.—six hours after midnight—so the appropriate figure is 1 minute (6×10 seconds). This is the A of your formula, which now reads:

7 hrs. 15 mins. $+ 6$ hrs. 0 mins. $+ 0$ hrs. 1 min. $+ $ or $ - R$

Table 1

Right: this table gives, in simplified form, Star Time for each day of every year that is not a leap year. Star Time is measured by the stars rather than the Sun.

	Jan.	Feb.	Mar.	April	May	June	July	Aug.	Sept.	Oct.	Nov.	Dec.
1	6 39	8 41	10 31	12 34	14 32	16 34	18 32	20 35	22 37	0 35	2 37	4 36
2	6 43	8 45	10 35	12 37	14 36	16 38	18 36	20 38	22 41	0 39	2 41	4 39
3	6 47	8 49	10 39	12 41	14 40	16 42	18 40	20 42	22 45	0 43	2 45	4 43
4	6 51	8 53	10 43	12 45	14 44	16 46	18 44	20 46	22 79	0 44	2 49	4 47
5	6 54	8 57	10 47	12 49	14 48	16 50	18 48	20 50	22 53	0 51	2 53	4 51
6	6 58	9 1	10 51	12 53	14 52	16 54	18 52	20 54	22 56	0 55	2 57	4 55
7	7 2	9 5	10 55	12 57	14 55	16 58	18 56	20 58	23 0	0 59	3 1	4 59
8	7 6	9 9	10 59	13 1	14 59	17 2	19 0	21 2	23 4	1 3	3 5	5 3
9	7 10	9 12	11 3	13 5	15 3	17 6	19 4	21 4	23 6	1 7	3 9	5 7
10	7 14	9 16	11 7	13 9	15 7	17 10	19 8	21 10	23 12	1 11	3 13	5 11
11	7 18	9 20	11 11	13 13	15 11	17 13	19 12	21 14	23 16	1 14	3 17	5 15
12	7 22	9 24	11 15	13 17	15 15	17 17	19 16	21 18	23 20	1 18	3 21	5 19
13	7 26	9 28	11 19	13 21	15 19	17 21	19 20	21 22	23 24	1 22	3 25	5 23
14	7 30	9 32	11 23	13 25	15 23	17 25	19 24	21 26	23 28	1 26	3 29	5 27
15	7 34	9 36	11 27	13 29	15 27	17 29	19 28	21 30	23 32	1 30	3 32	5 31
16	7 38	9 40	11 30	13 33	15 31	17 33	19 31	21 34	23 36	1 34	3 36	5 35
17	7 42	9 44	11 34	13 37	15 35	17 37	19 35	21 38	23 40	1 38	3 40	5 39
18	7 46	9 48	11 38	13 41	15 39	17 41	19 39	21 42	23 44	1 42	3 44	5 43
19	7 50	9 52	11 42	13 45	15 43	17 45	19 43	21 46	23 48	1 46	3 48	5 47
20	7 54	9 56	11 46	13 48	15 47	17 49	19 47	21 49	23 52	1 50	3 52	5 50
21	7 58	10 0	11 50	13 52	15 51	17 53	19 51	21 53	23 56	1 54	3 56	5 54
22	8 2	10 4	11 54	13 56	15 55	17 57	19 55	21 57	24 0	1 58	4 0	5 58
23	8 5	10 8	11 58	14 0	15 59	18 1	19 59	22 1	0 4	2 2	4 4	6 2
24	8 9	10 12	12 2	14 4	16 3	18 5	20 3	22 5	0 7	2 6	4 8	6 6
25	8 13	10 16	12 6	14 8	16 6	18 9	20 7	22 9	0 11	2 10	4 12	6 10
26	8 17	10 20	12 10	14 12	16 10	18 13	20 11	22 13	0 15	2 14	4 16	6 14
27	8 21	10 23	12 14	14 16	16 14	18 17	20 15	22 17	0 19	2 18	4 20	6 18
28	8 25	10 27	12 18	14 20	16 18	18 21	20 19	22 21	0 23	2 21	4 24	6 22
29	8 29		12 22	14 24	16 22	18 24	20 23	22 25	0 27	2 25	4 28	6 26
30	8 33		12 26	14 28	16 26	18 28	20 27	22 29	0 31	2 29	4 32	6 30
31	8 37		12 30		16 30		20 31	22 33		2 33		6 34

Note: Use this table as it stands for years 1902, 1906, 1910, 1914, 1918, 1922, 1927, 1931, 1935, 1939, 1943, 1947, 1951, 1955.

Deduct one minute from the time given for the years 1903, 1907, 1911, 1915, 1919, 1923.

Add one minute to the time given for the years 1901, 1905, 1909, 1913, 1917, 1921, 1925, 1926, 1930, 1934, 1938, 1942, 1946, 1950, 1954, 1959, 1963, 1967, 1971, 1975.

Add two minutes to the time given for the years 1900, 1929, 1933, 1937, 1941, 1945, 1949, 1953, 1957, 1958, 1962, 1966, 1970, 1974.

Add three minutes to the time given for the years 1961, 1965, 1969, 1973.

Table 2

Right: this table gives Star Time as applicable to leap years.

	Jan.	Feb.	Mar.	April	May	June	July	Aug.	Sept.	Oct.	Nov.	Dec.
1	6 38	8 40	10 34	12 37	14 35	16 37	18 35	20 38	22 40	0 38	2 40	4 39
2	6 42	8 44	10 38	12 40	14 39	16 41	18 39	20 41	22 44	0 42	2 44	4 42
3	6 46	8 48	10 42	12 44	14 43	16 45	18 43	20 45	22 48	0 46	2 48	4 46
4	6 50	8 52	10 46	12 48	14 47	16 49	18 47	20 49	22 52	0 50	2 52	4 50
5	6 54	8 56	10 50	12 52	14 51	16 53	18 51	20 53	22 56	0 54	2 56	4 54
6	6 57	9 0	10 54	12 56	14 55	16 57	18 55	20 57	22 59	0 58	3 0	4 58
7	7 1	9 4	10 58	13 0	14 56	17 1	18 59	21 1	23 3	1 2	3 4	5 2
8	7 5	9 8	11 2	13 4	15 2	17 5	19 3	21 5	23 7	1 6	3 8	5 6
9	7 9	9 12	11 6	13 8	15 6	17 9	19 7	21 9	23 11	1 10	3 12	5 10
10	7 13	9 15	11 10	13 12	15 10	17 13	19 11	21 13	23 15	1 14	3 16	5 14
11	7 17	9 19	11 14	13 16	15 14	17 16	19 15	21 17	23 19	1 17	3 20	5 18
12	7 21	9 23	11 18	13 20	15 18	17 20	19 19	21 21	23 23	1 21	3 24	5 22
13	7 25	9 27	11 22	13 24	15 22	17 24	19 23	21 25	23 27	1 25	3 28	5 26
14	7 29	9 31	11 26	13 28	15 26	17 27	19 27	21 29	23 31	1 29	3 32	5 30
15	7 33	9 35	11 30	13 32	15 30	17 32	19 31	21 33	23 35	1 33	3 35	5 34
16	7 37	9 39	11 33	13 36	15 34	17 36	19 34	21 37	23 39	1 37	3 39	5 38
17	7 41	9 43	11 37	13 40	15 38	17 40	19 38	21 41	23 43	1 41	3 43	5 42
18	7 45	9 47	11 41	13 44	15 42	17 44	19 42	21 45	23 47	1 45	3 47	5 46
19	7 49	9 51	11 45	13 48	15 46	17 48	19 46	21 49	23 51	1 49	3 51	5 50
20	7 53	9 55	11 49	13 51	15 50	17 52	19 50	21 52	23 55	1 53	3 55	5 53
21	7 57	9 59	11 53	13 55	15 54	17 56	19 54	21 56	23 59	1 57	3 59	5 57
22	8 1	10 3	11 57	13 59	15 58	18 0	19 58	22 0	0 3	2 1	4 3	6 1
23	8 5	10 7	12 1	14 3	16 2	18 4	20 2	22 4	0 7	2 5	4 7	6 5
24	8 8	10 11	12 5	14 7	16 6	18 8	20 6	22 8	0 10	2 9	4 11	6 9
25	8 12	10 15	12 9	14 11	16 9	18 12	20 10	22 12	0 14	2 13	4 15	6 13
26	8 16	10 19	12 13	14 15	16 13	18 16	20 14	22 16	0 18	2 17	4 19	6 17
27	8 20	10 22	12 17	14 19	16 17	18 20	20 18	22 20	0 22	2 21	4 23	6 21
28	8 24	10 26	12 21	14 23	16 21	18 23	20 22	22 24	0 26	2 24	4 27	6 25
29	8 28	10 30	12 25	14 27	16 25	18 27	20 26	22 28	0 30	2 28	4 31	6 29
30	8 32		12 29	14 31	16 29	18 31	20 30	22 32	0 34	2 32	4 35	6 33
31	8 36		12 33		16 33		20 34	22 36		2 36		6 37

Note: Use this table as it stands for the years 1924, 1928, 1932, 1936, 1940, 1944, 1948, 1952.

Deduct one minute from the time given for the years 1904, 1908, 1912, 1916, 1920.

Add one minute to the time given for the years 1956, 1960, 1964, 1968, 1972.

Table 3

Look at this table for time rectification—the R of the $S+T+A+$ or $-R$ formula for calculating your time of birth in Star Time. It lists most of the world's capitals and the major population centers of Britain and North America.

Location	R
Albany, New York	+ 5
Algiers	+12
Amarillo, Texas	−47
Amsterdam	−40
Athens	−25
Atlanta, Georgia	+22
Atlantic City, New Jersey	+ 2
Baghdad	− 2
Baker, Oregon	+ 9
Baltimore, Maryland	− 7
Bangor, Maine	+25
Bedford, England	− 2
Belgrade	+22
Berlin	− 6
Berne	−30
Birmingham, Alabama	+13
Birmingham, England	− 8
Bismarck, North Dakota	−43
Bogota	+ 3
Boise, Idaho	−45
Bonn	−32
Boston, England	0
Boston, Massachusetts	+16
Brussels	+17
Bucharest	−16
Budapest	+16
Buenos Aires	+ 7
Buffalo, New York	−16
Bury St. Edmunds, England	+ 3
Cairo	+ 5
Calgary, Alberta	−36
Cambridge, England	0
Canberra	− 3
Cape Town	−47
Caracas	+ 2
Cardiff, Wales	−13
Carlsbad, New Mexico	+ 3
Carlisle, England	−12
Charleston, South Carolina	−20
Charleston, West Virginia	−27
Charlotte, North Carolina	−23
Chelmsford, England	+ 2
Chester, England	−12
Cheyenne, Wyoming	+ 1
Chicago, Illinois	+ 9
Chichester, England	− 3
Cincinatti, Ohio	−38
Cleveland, Ohio	−27
Columbia, South Carolina	−24
Columbus, Ohio	−32
Copenhagen	−10
Dallas, Texas	−27
Delhi	−21
Denver, Colorado	0
Derby, England	− 6
Des Moines, Iowa	−15
Detroit, Michigan	−32
Dublin	−25
Dubuque, Iowa	− 3
Duluth, Minnesota	− 8
Durham, England	− 7
El Centro, California	+18
El Paso, Texas	− 6
Eugene, Oregon	−12
Fargo, North Dakota	−27
Fresno, California	+ 1
Glasgow, Scotland	−17
Gloucester, England	− 9
Grand Junction, Colorado	−14
Grand Rapids, Michigan	+17
Halifax, Nova Scotia	−14
Helena, Montana	−28
Helsinki	−24
Hereford, England	−11
Honolulu, Hawaii	−31
Huntingdon, England	− 1
Idaho Falls, Idaho	−28
Indianapolis, Indiana	+15
Ipswich, England	+ 5
Jackson, Mississippi	− 1
Jacksonville, Florida	−27
Jerusalem	+21
Kendal, England	−11
Key West, Florida	−27
Knoxville, Tennessee	+24
La Paz	−32
Las Vegas, Nevada	+19
Leeds, England	− 6
Leicester, England	− 5
Lima	− 8
Lincoln, England	− 2
Lincoln, Nebraska	−27
Lisbon	−37
Little Rock, Arkansas	− 8
London	0
Los Angeles, California	+ 7
Louisville, Kentucky	+17
Madrid	−15
Manchester, England	− 9
Manchester, New Hampshire	+14
Memphis, Tennessee	0
Mexico City	−36
Miami, Florida	−21
Milwaukee, Wisconsin	+ 8
Minneapolis, Minnesota	−13
Mobile, Alabama	+ 8
Montevideo	−15
Montgomery, Alabama	+15
Montpelier, Vermont	+10
Montreal, Quebec	+ 6
Moscow	+30
Nashville, Tennessee	+13
Newcastle, England	− 6
New Haven, Connecticut	+ 8
New Orleans, Louisiana	0
New York, New York	+ 4
Nome, Alaska	− 2
North Platte, Nebraska	−43
Oklahoma City, Oklahoma	−30
Oslo	−17
Ottawa, Ontario	− 3
Oxford, England	− 5
Paris	+ 9
Peking	−14
Philadelphia, Pennsylvania	− 1
Phoenix, Arizona	−28
Pierre, South Dakota	−41
Pittsburgh, Pennsylvania	−20
Port Arthur, Ontario	−57
Portland, Maine	+19
Portland, Oregon	−11
Prague	− 2
Providence, Rhode Island	+14
Quebec, Quebec	+15
Quito	−14
Raleigh, North Carolina	−15
Reading, England	− 4
Regina, Saskatchewan	+ 2
Reno, Nevada	+ 1
Richmond, Virginia	−10
Riga	−24
Rio de Janeiro	+ 7
Roanoke, Virginia	−20
Rome	−11
Sacramento, California	− 6
St. John, New Brunswick	−25
St. Louis, Missouri	− 1
Salt Lake City, Utah	−28
San Antonio, Texas	−34
San Diego, California	+11
San Francisco, California	−10
Santa Fe, New Mexico	− 4
Santiago	−43
Savannah, Georgia	−24
Scranton, Pennsylvania	− 3
Seattle, Washington	− 9
Shreveport, Louisiana	−15
Sioux Falls, South Dakota	−27
Singapore	−34
Sofia	−27
Spokane, Washington	+10
Springfield, Illinois	+ 1
Springfield, Massachusetts	+10
Springfield, Missouri	−13
Stockholm	+12
Syracuse, New York	− 5
Tampa, Florida	−30
Taunton, England	−13
Teheran	+27
Tokyo	+19
Toronto, Ontario	−18
Vancouver, British Columbia	−12
Victoria, British Columbia	−13
Vienna	+ 5
Wakefield, England	− 6
Warsaw	+24
Warwick, England	− 7
Washington, D.C.	− 8
Watertown, New York	− 4
Wellington	−21
Wichita, Kansas	−29
Wilmington, Delaware	− 2
Winnipeg, Manitoba	−29
Worcester, England	− 9
Yakima, Washington	− 2

R in the formula stands for "rectification"—the adjustment for the Zone Time of your birth because your birthplace lies east or west of the exact degree of longitude for which Zone Time is completely accurate.

In Table 3 opposite you will find a list of rectifications for most of the world's capital cities and the major North American and British population centers. If your birthplace, or a place close to it, does not appear in the table, you can easily work out the rectification for yourself using a good atlas in any reference library.

If you are making the calculation yourself, first find out from your atlas or local library the degrees of longitude at which the Zone Time for your birthplace is *exactly* correct. Then, from your atlas, count the number of degrees you were born east or west of that longitude. Convert these degrees into time simply by multiplying by four. If, for example, your birthplace was 5 degrees away from your Zone Time longitude, it would convert into time as 20 minutes. This 20 minutes would be your R figure in the formula. If you were born *west* of your Zone Time longitude this figure will be subtracted and is preceded by a minus sign. If your birthplace was *east*, R will be added and is therefore preceded by a plus sign.

To return to our example, we do not need to make any calculations for the person born in New York at 6 a.m. on January 10, 1934, since New York is one of the cities listed in Table 3. There we find that the R adjustment for New York is +4 minutes. So our formula now reads:

7 hrs. 15 mins. + 6 hrs. 0 mins. + 0 hrs. 1 min. + 0 hrs. 4 mins.

We now write the whole formula down as a simple addition:

S	7 hrs.	15 mins.
T	6 hrs.	0 mins.
A	0 hrs.	1 min.
R	0 hrs.	4 mins.
Star Time	13 hrs.	20 mins.

If the R figure happened to be a minus one it would, of course, be subtracted from the total of S + T + A.

Sometimes the calculation of Star Time results in a figure of more than 24 hours. When this happens, simply deduct 24 hours from the total to get the correct Star Time. If, for example, our final figure were not 13 hours 20 minutes but 33 hours 20 minutes, we would subtract 24 hours to give us a Star Time of 9 hours 20 minutes.

Following this process for your own time, date, and place of birth you will have arrived at the correct Star Time for your birth. The next step is to calculate the "Houses of Heaven"—the 12 divisions of the zodiac. Although there are 12 Houses just as there are 12 signs, the Houses are different from the signs and should not be confused with them.

Before calculating these Houses as they appear in your personal chart, it is important to note that there are many different methods of making this twelvefold division of the zodiac. All these methods have their supporters and their opponents; all have their advantages and disadvantages. The system of House division that we will be using was devised by the great 17th-century French astrologer Morin de Villefranche, often known as Morinus. His monumental work *Astrologia Gallica*, published in 1661, continues to exert a major influence on astrology.

To calculate the Houses of Heaven, turn to Table 4 on pages 115–118. The first column is a list of Star Times, and the other columns give the corresponding zodiac signs and degrees of the *cusps*—the dividing lines between each of the Houses. Before using the table you will need to know the conventional symbols astrologers use for the zodiac signs, which are the symbols that appear in Table 4. There is no need to memorize the symbols. A list of them, together with their corresponding zodiac signs, appears on pages 116–7. You can simply refer to this list as you consult the table.

Opposite each Star Time in the table is a list of the cusps, or divisions, between each of the first six of the twelve Houses. Returning to our example, we arrived at a Star Time of 13 hours 20 minutes. (This is underlined in red in the table). You will see from column one of the table that the first cusp corresponding to 13 hours 20 minutes is 21° 38′—that is, 21 degrees and 38 minutes. (Each degree is divided into 60 minutes.) This first cusp is 21° 38′ of Capricorn since the symbol for Capricorn appears above it at the top of column one. The second cusp is 22° 25′ of Aquarius. The third cusp is 20° 49′ of Pisces. The fourth is 18° 27′ of Aries. The fifth cusp is 17° 33′ of Taurus, and the sixth is 19° 7′ of Gemini. (Always be careful to move up the table from the line you are using to find the zodiac symbol you need—the one immediately above your line, not necessarily the one at the top of the column.)

We now write down the figures we have found for our first six cusps. For the purposes of our map it is sufficiently accurate to work to the nearest degree, so our list of cusps appears as follows:

Cusp 1   22° Capricorn
Cusp 2   22° Aquarius
Cusp 3   21° Pisces
Cusp 4   18° Aries
Cusp 5   18° Taurus
Cusp 6   19° Gemini

In our example, the exact Star Time of 13 hours 20 minutes is listed in the table. This will not always be the case. For instance, your Star Time might be 14 hours 22 minutes—a time which does not appear in the table. In this case you simply take the two listed Star Times nearest to your own and work out your cusp positions from these. The two listed times nearest to 14 hours 22 minutes are 14 hours 20 minutes and 14 hours 24 minutes. At 14 hours 20 minutes the first cusp is 7° 21′ Aquarius, and at 14 hours 24 minutes it is 8° 23′ Aquarius. The cusp position at 14 hours 22 minutes would clearly be halfway between these two positions, so your first cusp will be Aquarius 7° 21′. (There are 60 minutes to a degree. The difference between 7° 21′ and 8° 23′ is 1° 2′; half of 1° 2′ is 31′; 7° 21′ + 31′ is 7° 52′.) You can obtain the other five cusp positions by the same process.

Now the time has come to insert your six cusp positions on a map of the zodiac. Draw your map like the diagram on page 119 with the 12 cusps, or dividing lines between the houses, marked on it. On page 120 you will see the map with the first six cusp

Table 4

This table gives the degrees on the cusps for each four-minute interval of Star Time for use on a Morinus chart. Such a chart divides the Houses according to the system of the 17th-century astrologer known as Morinus.

S.T.	1	2	3	4	5	6
0 0	0 ♋ 0	2 ♌ 11	2 ♍ 5	0 ♎ 0	27 ♎ 55	27 ♏ 49
0 4	1 5	3 13	3 3	0 55	28 53	28 52
0 8	2 11	4 16	4 0	1 50	29 49	29 54
0 12	3 16	5 18	4 57	2 45	0 ♏ 47	0 ♐ 57
0 16	4 22	6 20	5 54	3 40	1 45	2 0
0 20	5 27	7 21	6 50	4 35	2 43	3 3
0 24	6 32	8 23	7 47	5 31	3 41	4 7
0 28	7 37	9 24	8 43	6 26	4 39	5 10
0 32	8 43	10 25	9 40	7 21	5 38	6 14
0 36	9 48	11 26	10 36	8 16	6 36	7 18
0 40	10 53	12 27	11 33	9 11	7 35	8 22
0 44	11 58	13 27	12 28	10 7	8 34	9 26
0 48	13 3	14 28	13 24	11 2	9 33	10 30
0 52	14 7	15 28	14 20	11 57	10 33	11 34
0 56	15 12	16 28	15 16	12 53	11 32	12 39
1 0	16 17	17 28	16 11	13 49	12 32	13 43
1 4	17 21	18 28	17 7	14 44	13 32	14 48
1 8	18 26	19 27	18 3	15 40	14 32	15 52
1 12	19 30	20 27	18 58	16 36	15 32	16 57
1 16	20 34	21 26	19 53	17 32	16 33	18 2
1 20	21 38	22 25	20 49	18 27	17 33	19 7
1 24	22 42	23 24	21 43	19 24	18 34	20 12
1 28	23 46	24 22	22 39	20 20	19 35	21 17
1 32	24 50	25 21	23 34	21 17	20 36	22 23
1 36	25 53	26 19	24 29	22 13	21 37	23 20
1 40	26 57	27 17	25 25	23 10	22 39	24 33
1 44	28 0	28 15	26 20	24 6	23 40	25 38
1 48	29 3	29 13	27 15	25 3	24 42	26 44
1 52	0 ♌ 6	0 ♍ 11	28 10	26 0	25 44	27 49
1 56	1 8	1 7	29 5	26 57	26 47	28 55
2 0	2 ♌ 11	2 ♍ 5	0 ♎ 0	27 ♎ 55	27 ♏ 49	0 ♑ 0
2 4	3 13	3 3	0 55	28 53	28 52	1 5
2 8	4 16	4 0	1 50	29 49	29 54	2 11
2 12	5 18	4 57	2 45	0 ♏ 47	0 ♐ 57	3 16
2 16	6 20	5 54	3 40	1 45	2 0	4 22
2 20	7 21	6 50	4 35	2 43	3 3	5 27
2 24	8 23	7 47	5 31	3 41	4 7	6 32
2 28	9 24	8 43	6 26	4 39	5 10	7 37
2 32	10 25	9 40	7 21	5 38	6 14	8 43
2 36	11 26	10 36	8 16	6 36	7 18	9 48
2 40	12 27	11 33	9 11	7 35	8 22	10 53
2 44	13 27	12 28	10 7	8 34	9 26	11 58
2 48	14 28	13 24	11 2	9 33	10 30	13 3
2 52	15 28	14 20	11 57	10 33	11 34	14 7
2 56	16 28	15 16	12 53	11 32	12 39	15 12
3 0	17 28	16 11	13 49	12 32	13 43	16 17
3 4	18 28	17 7	14 44	13 32	14 48	17 21
3 8	19 27	18 3	15 40	14 32	15 52	18 26
3 12	20 27	18 58	16 36	15 32	16 57	19 30
3 16	21 26	19 53	17 32	16 33	18 2	20 34
3 20	22 25	20 49	18 27	17 33	19 7	21 38
3 24	23 24	21 43	19 24	18 34	20 12	22 42
3 28	24 22	22 39	20 20	19 35	21 17	23 46
3 32	25 21	23 34	21 17	20 36	22 23	24 50
3 36	26 19	24 29	22 13	21 37	23 28	25 53
3 40	27 17	25 25	23 10	22 39	24 33	26 57
3 44	28 15	26 20	24 6	23 40	25 38	28 0
3 48	29 13	27 15	25 3	24 42	26 44	29 3
3 52	0 ♍ 11	28 10	26 0	25 44	27 49	0 ♒ 6
3 56	1 7	29 5	26 57	26 47	28 55	1 8
4 0	2 ♍ 5	0 ♎ 0	27 ♎ 55	27 ♏ 49	0 ♑ 0	2 ♒ 11
4 4	3 3	0 55	28 53	28 52	1 5	3 13
4 8	4 0	1 50	29 49	29 54	2 11	4 16
4 12	4 57	2 45	0 ♏ 47	0 ♐ 57	3 16	5 18
4 16	5 54	3 40	1 45	2 0	4 22	6 20
4 20	6 50	4 35	2 43	3 3	5 27	7 21
4 24	7 47	5 31	3 41	4 7	6 32	8 23
4 28	8 43	6 26	4 39	5 10	7 37	9 24
4 32	9 40	7 21	5 38	6 14	8 43	10 25
4 36	10 36	8 16	6 36	7 18	9 48	11 26
4 40	11 33	9 11	7 35	8 22	10 53	12 27
4 44	12 28	10 7	8 34	9 26	11 58	13 27
4 48	13 24	11 2	9 33	10 30	13 3	14 28
4 52	14 20	11 57	10 33	11 34	14 7	15 28
4 56	15 16	12 53	11 32	12 39	15 12	16 28
5 0	16 11	13 49	12 32	13 43	16 17	17 28
5 4	17 7	14 44	13 32	14 48	17 21	18 28
5 8	18 3	15 40	14 32	15 52	18 26	19 27
5 12	18 58	16 36	15 32	16 57	19 30	20 27
5 16	19 53	17 32	16 33	18 2	20 34	21 26
5 20	20 49	18 27	17 33	19 7	21 38	22 25
5 24	21 43	19 24	18 34	20 12	22 42	23 24
5 28	22 39	20 20	19 35	21 17	23 46	24 22
5 32	23 34	21 17	20 36	22 23	24 50	25 21
5 36	24 29	22 13	21 37	23 28	25 53	26 19
5 40	25 25	23 10	22 39	24 33	26 57	27 17
5 44	26 20	24 6	23 40	25 38	28 0	28 15
5 48	27 15	25 3	24 42	26 44	29 3	29 13
5 52	28 10	26 0	25 44	27 49	0 ♒ 6	0 ♓ 11
5 56	29 5	26 57	26 47	28 55	1 8	1 7

Aries ♈

Taurus ♉

Gemini ♊

Cancer ♋

Leo ♌

Virgo ♍

S.T.	1	2	3	4	5	6
6 0	0 ≏ 0	27 ≏ 55	27 ♏ 49	0 ♑ 0	2 ♒ 11	2 ♓ 5
6 4	0 55	28 53	28 52	1 5	3 13	3 3
6 8	1 50	29 49	29 54	2 11	4 16	4 0
6 12	2 45	0 ♏ 47	0 ♐ 57	3 16	5 18	4 57
6 16	3 40	1 45	2 0	4 22	6 20	5 54
6 20	4 35	2 43	3 3	5 27	7 21	6 50
6 24	5 31	3 41	4 7	6 32	8 23	7 47
6 28	6 26	4 39	5 10	7 37	9 24	8 43
6 32	7 21	5 38	6 14	8 43	10 25	9 40
6 36	8 16	6 36	7 18	9 48	11 26	10 36
6 40	9 11	7 35	8 22	10 53	12 27	11 33
6 44	10 7	8 34	9 26	11 58	13 27	12 28
6 48	11 2	9 33	10 30	13 3	14 28	13 24
6 52	11 57	10 33	11 34	14 7	15 28	14 20
6 56	12 53	11 32	12 39	15 12	16 28	15 16
7 0	13 49	12 32	13 43	16 17	17 28	16 11
7 4	14 44	13 32	14 48	17 21	18 28	17 7
7 8	15 40	14 32	15 52	18 26	19 27	18 3
7 12	16 36	15 32	16 57	19 30	20 27	18 58
7 16	17 32	16 33	18 2	20 34	21 26	19 53
7 20	18 27	17 33	19 7	21 38	22 25	20 49
7 24	19 24	18 34	20 12	22 42	23 24	21 43
7 28	20 20	19 35	21 17	23 46	24 22	22 39
7 32	21 17	20 36	22 23	24 50	25 21	23 34
7 36	22 13	21 37	23 28	25 53	26 19	24 29
7 40	23 10	22 39	24 33	26 57	27 17	25 25
7 44	24 6	23 40	25 38	28 0	28 15	26 20
7 48	25 3	24 42	26 44	29 3	29 13	27 15
7 52	26 0	25 44	27 49	0 ♒ 6	0 ♓ 11	28 10
7 56	26 57	26 47	28 55	1 8	1 7	29 5
8 0	27 ≏ 55	27 ♏ 49	0 ♑ 0	2 ♒ 11	2 ♓ 5	0 ♈ 0
8 4	28 53	28 52	1 5	3 13	3 3	0 55
8 8	29 49	29 54	2 11	4 16	4 0	1 50
8 12	0 ♏ 47	0 ♐ 57	3 16	5 18	4 57	2 45
8 16	1 45	2 0	4 22	6 20	5 54	3 40
8 20	2 43	3 3	5 27	7 21	6 50	4 35
8 24	3 41	4 7	6 32	8 23	7 47	5 31
8 28	4 39	5 10	7 37	9 24	8 43	6 26
8 32	5 38	6 14	8 43	10 25	9 40	7 21
8 36	6 36	7 18	9 48	11 26	10 36	8 16
8 40	7 35	8 22	10 53	12 27	11 33	9 11
8 44	8 34	9 26	11 58	13 27	12 28	10 7
8 48	9 33	10 30	13 3	14 28	13 24	11 2
8 52	10 33	11 34	14 7	15 28	14 20	11 57
8 56	11 32	12 39	15 12	16 28	15 16	12 53
9 0	12 32	13 43	16 17	17 28	16 11	13 49
9 4	13 32	14 48	17 21	18 28	17 7	14 44
9 8	14 32	15 52	18 26	19 27	18 3	15 40
9 12	15 32	16 57	19 30	20 27	18 58	16 36
9 16	16 33	18 2	20 34	21 26	19 53	17 32
9 20	17 33	19 7	21 38	22 25	20 49	18 27
9 24	18 34	20 12	22 42	23 24	21 43	19 24
9 28	19 35	21 17	23 46	24 22	22 39	20 20
9 32	20 36	22 23	24 50	25 21	23 34	21 17
9 36	21 37	23 28	25 53	26 19	24 29	22 13
9 40	22 39	24 33	26 57	27 17	25 25	23 10
9 44	23 40	25 38	28 0	28 15	26 20	24 6
9 48	24 42	26 44	29 3	29 13	27 15	25 3
9 52	25 44	27 49	0 ♒ 6	0 ♓ 11	28 10	26 0
9 56	26 47	28 55	1 8	1 7	29 5	26 57
10 0	27 ♏ 49	0 ♑ 0	2 ♒ 11	2 ♓ 5	0 ♈ 0	27 ♈ 55
10 4	28 52	1 5	3 13	3 3	0 55	28 53
10 8	29 54	2 11	4 16	4 0	1 50	29 49
10 12	0 ♐ 57	3 16	5 18	4 57	2 45	0 ♉ 47
10 16	2 0	4 22	6 20	5 54	3 40	1 45
10 20	3 3	5 27	7 21	6 50	4 35	2 43
10 24	4 7	6 32	8 23	7 47	5 31	3 41
10 28	5 10	7 37	9 24	8 43	6 26	4 39
10 32	6 14	8 43	10 25	9 40	7 21	5 38
10 36	7 18	9 48	11 26	10 36	8 16	6 36
10 40	8 22	10 53	12 27	11 33	9 11	7 35
10 44	9 26	11 58	13 27	12 28	10 7	8 34
10 48	10 30	13 3	14 28	13 24	11 2	9 33
10 52	11 34	14 7	15 28	14 20	11 57	10 33
10 56	12 39	15 12	16 28	15 16	12 53	11 32
11 0	13 43	16 17	17 29	16 11	13 49	12 32
11 4	14 48	17 21	18 28	17 7	14 44	13 32
11 8	15 52	18 26	19 27	18 3	15 40	14 32
11 12	16 57	19 30	20 27	18 58	16 36	15 32
11 16	18 2	20 34	21 26	19 53	17 32	16 33
11 20	19 7	21 38	22 25	20 49	18 27	17 33
11 24	20 12	22 42	23 24	21 43	19 24	18 34
11 28	21 17	23 46	24 22	22 39	20 20	19 35
11 32	22 23	24 50	25 21	23 34	21 17	20 36
11 36	23 23	25 53	26 19	24 29	22 13	21 37
11 40	24 33	26 57	27 17	25 25	23 10	22 39
11 44	25 38	28 0	28 15	26 20	24 6	23 40
11 48	26 44	29 3	29 13	27 15	25 3	24 42
11 52	27 49	0 ♒ 6	0 ♓ 11	28 10	26 0	25 44
11 56	28 55	1 8	1 7	29 5	26 57	26 47

S.T.	1		2		3		4		5		6	
12 0	0 ♑	0	2 ♒	11	2 ♓	5	0 ♈	0	27 ♈	55	27 ♉	49
12 4	1	5	3	13	3	3	0	55	28	53	28	52
12 8	2	11	4	16	4	0	1	50	29	49	29	54
12 12	3	16	5	18	4	57	2	45	0 ♉	47	0 ♊	57
12 16	4	22	6	20	5	54	3	40	1	45	2	0
12 20	5	27	7	21	6	50	4	35	2	43	3	3
12 24	6	32	8	23	7	47	5	31	3	41	4	7
12 28	7	37	9	24	8	43	6	26	4	39	5	10
12 32	8	43	10	25	9	40	7	21	5	38	6	14
12 36	9	48	11	26	10	36	8	16	6	36	7	18
12 40	10	53	12	27	11	33	9	11	7	35	8	22
12 44	11	58	13	27	12	28	10	7	8	34	9	26
12 48	13	3	14	28	13	24	11	2	9	33	10	30
12 52	14	7	15	28	14	20	11	57	10	33	11	34
12 56	15	12	16	28	15	16	12	53	11	32	12	39
13 0	16	17	17	28	16	11	13	49	12	32	13	43
13 4	17	21	18	28	17	7	14	44	13	32	14	48
13 8	18	26	19	27	18	3	15	40	14	32	15	52
13 12	19	30	20	27	18	58	16	36	15	32	16	57
13 16	20	34	21	26	19	53	17	32	16	33	18	2
13 20	21	38	22	25	20	49	18	27	17	33	19	7
13 24	22	42	23	24	21	43	19	24	18	34	20	12
13 28	23	46	24	22	22	39	20	20	19	35	21	17
13 32	24	50	25	21	23	34	21	17	20	36	22	23
13 36	25	53	26	19	24	29	22	13	21	37	23	28
13 40	26	57	27	17	25	25	23	10	22	39	24	33
13 44	28	0	28	15	26	20	24	6	23	40	25	38
13 48	29	3	29	13	27	15	25	3	24	42	26	44
13 52	0 ♒	6	0 ♓	11	28	10	26	0	25	44	27	49
13 56	1	8	1	7	29	5	26	57	26	47	28	55
14 0	2 ♒	11	2 ♓	5	0 ♈	0	27 ♈	55	27 ♉	49	0 ♋	0
14 4	3	13	3	3	0	55	28	53	28	52	1	5
14 8	4	16	4	0	1	50	29	49	29	54	2	11
14 12	5	18	4	57	2	45	0 ♉	47	0 ♊	57	3	16
14 16	6	20	5	54	3	40	1	45	2	0	4	22
14 20	7	21	6	50	4	35	2	43	3	3	5	27
14 24	8	23	7	47	5	31	3	41	4	7	6	32
14 28	9	24	8	43	6	26	4	39	5	10	7	37
14 32	10	25	9	40	7	21	5	38	6	14	8	43
14 36	11	26	10	36	8	16	6	36	7	18	9	49
14 40	12	27	11	33	9	11	7	35	8	22	10	53
14 44	13	27	12	28	10	7	8	34	9	26	11	58
14 48	14	28	13	24	11	2	9	33	10	30	13	3
14 52	15	28	14	20	11	57	10	33	11	34	14	7
14 56	16	28	15	16	12	53	11	32	12	39	15	12
15 0	17	28	16	11	13	49	12	32	13	43	16	17
15 4	18	28	17	7	14	44	13	32	14	48	17	21
15 8	19	27	18	3	15	40	14	32	15	52	18	26
15 12	20	27	18	58	16	36	15	32	16	57	19	30
15 16	21	26	19	53	17	32	16	33	18	2	20	34
15 20	22	25	20	49	18	27	17	33	19	7	21	38
15 24	23	24	21	43	19	24	18	34	20	12	22	42
15 28	24	22	22	39	20	20	19	35	21	17	23	46
15 32	25	21	23	34	21	17	20	36	22	23	24	50
15 36	26	19	24	29	22	13	21	37	23	28	25	53
15 40	27	17	25	25	23	10	22	39	24	33	26	57
15 44	28	15	26	20	24	6	23	40	25	38	28	0
15 48	29	13	27	15	25	3	24	42	26	44	29	3
15 52	0 ♓	11	28	10	26	0	25	44	27	49	0 ♌	6
15 56	1	7	29	5	26	57	26	47	28	55	1	8
16 0	2 ♓	5	0 ♈	0	27 ♈	55	27 ♉	49	0 ♋	0	2 ♌	11
16 4	3	3	0	55	28	53	28	52	1	5	3	13
16 8	4	0	1	50	29	49	29	54	2	11	4	16
16 12	4	57	2	45	0 ♉	47	0 ♊	57	3	16	5	19
16 16	5	54	3	40	1	45	2	0	4	22	6	20
16 20	6	50	4	35	2	43	3	3	5	27	7	21
16 24	7	47	5	31	3	41	4	7	6	32	8	23
16 28	8	43	6	26	4	39	5	10	7	37	9	24
16 32	9	40	7	21	5	38	6	14	8	43	10	25
16 36	10	36	8	16	6	36	7	18	9	48	11	26
16 40	11	33	9	11	7	35	8	22	10	53	12	27
16 44	12	28	10	7	8	34	9	26	11	58	13	27
16 48	13	24	11	2	9	33	10	30	13	3	14	28
16 52	14	20	11	57	10	33	11	34	14	7	15	28
16 56	15	16	12	53	11	32	12	39	15	12	16	28
17 0	16	11	13	49	12	32	13	43	16	17	17	28
17 4	17	7	14	44	13	32	14	48	17	21	18	28
17 8	18	3	15	40	14	32	15	52	18	26	19	27
17 12	18	58	16	36	15	32	16	57	19	30	20	27
17 16	19	53	17	32	16	33	18	2	20	34	21	26
17 20	20	49	18	27	17	33	19	7	21	38	22	25
17 24	21	43	19	24	18	34	20	12	22	42	23	24
17 28	22	39	20	20	19	35	21	17	23	46	24	22
17 32	23	34	21	17	20	36	22	23	24	50	25	21
17 36	24	29	22	13	21	37	23	28	25	53	26	19
17 40	25	25	23	10	22	39	24	33	26	57	27	17
17 44	26	20	24	6	23	40	25	38	28	0	28	15
17 48	27	15	25	3	24	42	26	44	29	3	29	13
17 52	28	10	26	0	25	44	27	49	0 ♌	6	0 ♍	11
17 56	29	5	26	57	26	47	28	55	1	8	1	7

Libra

Scorpio

Sagittarius

Capricorn

Aquarius

Pisces

S.T.	1	2	3	4	5	6
18 0	0 ♈ 0	27 ♈ 55	27 ♉ 49	0 ♋ 0	2 ♌ 11	2 ♍ 5
18 4	0 55	28 53	28 52	1 5	3 13	3 3
18 8	1 50	29 49	29 54	2 11	4 16	4 0
18 12	2 45	0 ♉ 47	0 ♊ 57	3 16	5 18	4 57
18 16	3 40	1 45	2 0	4 22	6 20	5 54
18 20	4 35	2 43	3 3	5 27	7 21	6 50
18 24	5 31	3 41	4 7	6 32	8 23	7 47
18 28	6 26	4 39	5 10	7 37	9 24	8 43
18 32	7 21	5 38	6 14	8 43	10 25	9 40
18 36	8 16	6 36	7 18	9 48	11 26	10 36
18 40	9 11	7 35	8 22	10 53	12 27	11 33
18 44	10 7	8 34	9 26	11 58	13 27	12 28
18 48	11 2	9 33	10 30	13 3	14 28	13 24
18 52	11 57	10 33	11 34	14 7	15 28	14 20
18 56	12 53	11 32	12 39	15 12	16 28	15 16
19 0	13 49	12 32	13 43	16 17	17 28	16 11
19 4	14 44	13 32	14 48	17 21	18 28	17 7
19 8	15 40	14 32	15 52	18 26	19 27	18 3
19 12	16 36	15 32	16 57	19 30	20 27	18 58
19 16	17 32	16 33	18 2	20 34	21 26	19 53
19 20	18 27	17 33	19 7	21 38	22 25	20 49
19 24	19 24	18 34	20 12	22 42	23 24	21 43
19 28	20 20	19 35	21 17	23 46	24 22	22 39
19 32	21 17	20 36	22 23	24 50	25 21	23 34
19 36	22 13	21 37	23 28	25 53	26 19	24 29
19 40	23 10	22 39	24 33	26 57	27 17	25 25
19 44	24 6	23 40	25 38	28 0	28 15	26 20
19 48	25 3	24 42	26 44	29 3	29 13	27 15
19 52	26 0	25 44	27 49	0 ♌ 6	0 ♍ 11	28 10
19 56	26 57	26 47	28 55	1 8	1 7	29 5
20 0	27 ♈ 55	27 ♉ 49	0 ♋ 0	2 ♌ 11	2 ♍ 5	0 ♎ 0
20 4	28 53	28 52	1 5	3 13	3 3	0 55
20 8 •	29 49	29 54	2 11	4 16	4 0	1 50
20 12	0 ♉ 47	0 ♊ 57	3 16	5 18	4 57	2 45
20 16	1 45	2 0	4 22	6 20	5 54	3 40
20 20	2 43	3 3	5 27	7 21	6 50	4 35
20 24	3 41	4 7	6 32	8 23	7 47	5 31
20 28	4 39	5 10	7 37	9 24	8 43	6 26
20 32	5 38	6 14	8 43	10 25	9 40	7 21
20 36	6 36	7 18	9 48	11 26	10 36	8 16
20 40	7 35	8 22	10 53	12 27	11 33	9 11
20 44	8 34	9 26	11 58	13 27	12 28	10 7
20 48	9 33	10 30	13 3	14 28	13 24	11 2
20 52	10 33	11 34	14 7	15 28	14 20	11 57
20 56	11 32	12 39	15 12	16 28	15 16	12 52
21 0	12 32	13 43	16 17	17 28	16 11	13 49
21 4	13 32	14 48	17 21	18 28	17 7	14 44
21 8	14 32	15 52	18 26	19 27	18 3	15 40
21 12	15 32	16 57	19 30	20 27	18 58	16 36
21 16	16 33	18 2	20 34	21 26	19 53	17 32
21 20	17 33	19 7	21 38	22 25	20 49	18 27
21 24	18 34	20 12	22 42	23 24	21 43	19 24
21 28	19 35	21 17	23 46	24 22	22 39	20 20
21 32	20 36	22 23	24 50	25 21	23 34	21 17
21 36	21 37	23 28	25 53	26 19	24 29	22 13
21 40	22 39	24 33	26 57	27 17	25 25	23 10
21 44	23 40	25 38	28 0	28 15	26 20	24 6
21 48	24 42	26 44	29 3	29 13	27 15	25 3
21 52	25 44	27 49	0 ♌ 6	0 ♍ 11	28 10	26 0
21 56	26 47	28 55	1 8	1 7	29 5	26 57
22 0	27 ♉ 49	0 ♋ 0	2 ♌ 11	2 ♍ 5	0 ♎ 0	27 ♎ 55
22 4	28 52	1 5	3 13	3 3	0 55	28 53
22 8	29 54	2 11	4 16	4 0	1 50	29 49
22 12	0 ♊ 57	3 16	5 18	4 57	2 45	0 ♏ 47
22 16	2 0	4 22	6 20	5 54	3 40	1 45
22 20	3 3	5 27	7 21	6 50	4 35	2 43
22 24	4 7	6 32	8 23	7 47	5 31	3 41
22 28	5 10	7 37	9 24	8 43	6 26	4 39
22 32	6 14	8 43	10 25	9 40	7 21	5 38
22 36	7 18	9 48	11 26	10 36	8 16	6 36
22 40	8 22	10 53	12 27	11 33	9 11	7 35
22 44	9 26	11 58	13 27	12 28	10 7	8 34
22 48	10 30	13 3	14 28	13 24	11 2	9 33
22 52	11 34	14 7	15 28	14 20	11 57	10 33
22 56	12 39	15 12	16 28	15 16	12 53	11 32
23 0	13 43	16 17	17 28	16 11	13 49	12 32
23 4	14 48	17 21	18 28	17 7	14 44	13 32
23 8	15 52	18 26	19 27	18 3	15 40	14 32
23 12	16 57	19 30	20 27	18 58	16 36	15 32
23 16	18 2	20 34	21 25	19 53	17 32	16 33
23 20	19 7	21 38	22 25	20 49	18 27	17 33
23 24	20 12	22 42	23 24	21 43	19 24	18 34
23 28	21 17	23 46	24 22	22 39	20 20	19 35
23 32	22 23	24 50	25 21	23 34	21 17	20 36
23 36	23 28	25 53	26 19	24 29	22 13	21 37
23 40	24 33	26 57	27 17	25 25	23 10	22 39
23 44	25 30	28 0	28 15	26 20	24 6	23 40
23 48	26 44	29 3	29 13	27 15	25 3	24 42
23 52	27 49	0 ♌ 6	0 ♍ 11	28 10	26 0	25 44
23 56	28 55	1 8	1 7	29 5	26 57	26 47
24 0	0 ♋ 0	2 11	2 5	0 ♎ 0	27 55	27 49

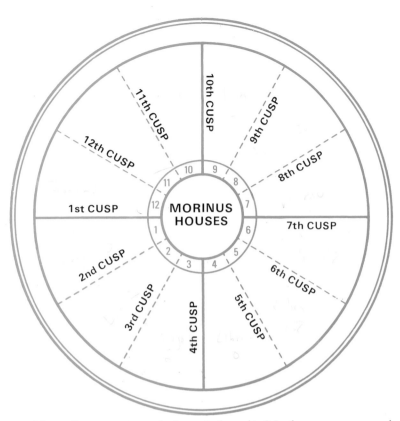

Right: a blank Morinus chart ready to have the zodiacal degrees inserted on the cusps.

positions for our example inserted on it. Mark your cusp positions in the same way.

Now you need to find and insert the zodiacal signs and degrees for the other six cusps. This is easily done, for each of these cusps has the same degrees but the opposite sign of the zodiac to the cusp immediately opposite it on the map. The opposites for each sign on the zodiac are listed below.

Sign	Opposite Sign
Aries	Libra
Taurus	Scorpio
Gemini	Sagittarius
Cancer	Capricorn
Leo	Aquarius
Virgo	Pisces
Libra	Aries
Scorpio	Taurus
Sagittarius	Gemini
Capricorn	Cancer
Aquarius	Leo
Pisces	Virgo

So for our example we can now make a list of cusps seven to 12—remember the *same degrees* but the *opposite signs*.

Cusp	7	22° Cancer
Cusp	8	22° Leo
Cusp	9	21° Virgo
Cusp	10	18° Libra
Cusp	11	18° Scorpio
Cusp	12	19° Sagittarius

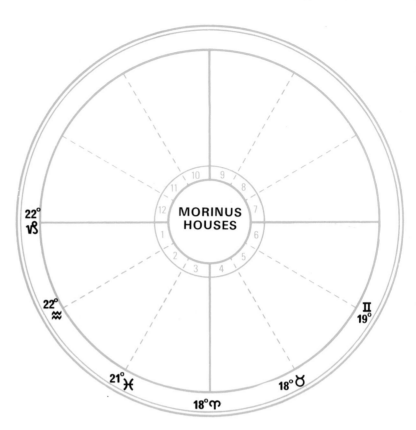

22°
♑

22°
♒

22°
♓ 21°

18° ♈

18° ♉

♊ 19°

MORINUS
HOUSES

Right: a Morinus chart with the
zodiacal degrees inserted on the
cusps of the first six Houses.

Then mark these positions on our map (see diagram page 121).

You will already have noticed that the 12 cusps go around the
chart in counterclockwise order. Therefore the sign and degree
of the first cusp—22° Capricorn in our example—appears at the
position corresponding to nine o'clock on a watch, and the sign
and degree of the second cusp—22° Aquarius in our example—
comes at the eight o'clock, not the ten o'clock, position. The sign
for the third cusp appears at the seven o'clock position, and so on.

The cusps divide off the 12 Houses. The First House therefore
covers the section from the first cusp (22° Capricorn) to the
second cusp (22° Aquarius), the Second House lies between the
second cusp (22° Aquarius) and the third cusp (21° Pisces), and
so on counterclockwise around the circle.

The degree on our first cusp is the 22° of Capricorn. But remember that each sign occupies 30° of the zodiac circle. This
means that the first 22 degrees of Capricorn are in the *Twelfth
House*, and only the remaining eight degrees of that sign are in
the First House. Similarly, in our example, 22 degrees of Aquarius are in the First House and only eight in the Second House,
and so on round to the last sign, Sagittarius, which has 19 degrees
in the Eleventh House and 11 degrees in the Twelfth House.

The final step in constructing your chart is to insert the position of the Sun. Table 5 on page 122 shows the Sun's position to
the nearest degree for every day of the year. These positions are
for midnight at Greenwich, England—the point from which all
degrees of longitude, East or West, are measured. In order to find
the Sun's position when you were born, therefore, you will need
to translate your local time of birth into Greenwich Mean Time.
Your local library should be able to tell you how much your local

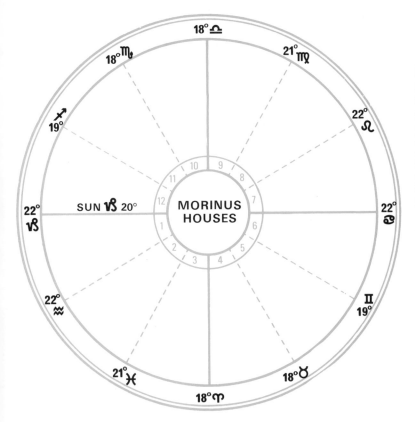

Left: a Morinus chart with the zodiacal degrees inserted on the cusps of all 12 Houses, and the Sun placed in its House position. Notice that the zodiacal degrees on the cusps of Houses 7–12 are exactly six Houses from those on cusps 1–6. Sometimes more than one House is ruled by the same sign. An example of this is provided by the map of General Gordon on page 129, where Aries rules the First and Second Houses and Libra both the Seventh and Eighth Houses. In such cases certain signs do not rule any house, and these are known as "intercepted signs." In General Gordon's map the intercepted signs are Gemini and Sagittarius. If you have intercepted signs on your own map, mark them in the same way as they are on General Gordon's map.

time is ahead of, or behind, Greenwich Mean Time. If your Greenwich time of birth is *before* noon simply use the Sun position shown in Table 5 for your date of birth. If your Greenwich time of birth is *after* 12 noon, use the Sun positions for the day *following* your birth date.

In our example, the person was born in New York on January 10, 1934 at 6 a.m. New York uses Eastern Standard Time which is five hours behind Greenwich. So, according to Greenwich Mean Time, the person was born at 11 a.m., or eleven o'clock in the morning on January 10. We can therefore use the Sun position on the date of birth as shown in Table 5. If the person had been born at 6 *p.m.* rather than 6 a.m., the Greenwich time of birth would have been eleven o'clock in the evening, so we would have used the Sun position for the following day, January 11.

The Sun position for January 10 (see Table 5 on next page) is 20° Capricorn. We therefore insert this on our map of the zodiac as shown in the map above. Your own Sun position should be marked in the same way in the relevant House on your chart.

In our example the Sun (positioned at 20° Capricorn) is inserted in the Twelfth House. This is because the degree and sign on the cusp between the Twelfth and First Houses is the 22° of Capricorn and the first 22 degrees of Capricorn therefore lie in the Twelfth House.

To insert your Sun in the correct House, first find the cusp sign that corresponds to the sign given for your Sun position. Then, if the number of degrees given for your Sun are *lower* than those of the particular cusp sign, the Sun goes in the House *before* that

Table 5

These simplified charts show the Sun's position in the zodiac for each day in the ordinary year (top) and in leap year (bottom).

Ordinary Years

	Jan.	Feb.	Mar.	April	May	June	July	Aug.	Sept.	Oct.	Nov.	Dec.
1	10 ♑	12 ♒	10 ♓	11 ♈	10 ♉	11 ♊	9 ♋	8 ♌	8 ♍	7 ♎	8 ♏	9 ♐
2	11	13	11	12	11	11	10	9	9	8	9	10
3	12	14	12	13	12	12	11	10	10	9	10	11
4	13	15	13	14	13	13	12	11	11	10	11	12
5	14	16	14	15	14	14	13	12	12	11	12	13
6	15	17	15	16	15	15	14	13	13	12	13	14
7	16	18	16	17	16	16	14	14	14	13	14	15
8	17	19	17	18	17	17	15	15	15	14	15	16
9	18	20	18	19	18	18	16	16	16	15	16	17
10	20	21	19	20	19	19	17	17	17	16	17	18
11	21	22	20	21	20	20	18	18	18	17	18	19
12	22	23	21	22	21	21	19	19	19	18	19	20
13	23	24	22	23	22	22	20	20	20	19	20	21
14	24	25	23	24	23	23	21	21	21	20	21	22
15	25	26	24	25	24	23	22	22	22	21	22	23
16	26	27	25	26	25	24	23	23	23	22	23	24
17	27	28	26	27	26	25	24	24	24	23	24	25
18	28	29	27	28	27	26	25	25	25	24	25	26
19	29	0 ♓	28	29	28	27	26	26	26	25	26	27
20	0 ♒	1	29	0 ♉	29	28	27	27	27	26	27	28
21	1	2	0 ♈	1	0 ♊	29	28	28	28	27	28	29
22	2	3	1	2	1	0 ♋	29	29	29	28	29	0 ♑
23	3	4	2	2	1	1	0 ♌	29	0 ♎	29	0 ♐	1
24	4	5	3	3	2	2	1	0 ♍	1	0 ♏	1	2
25	5	6	4	4	3	3	2	1	2	1	2	3
26	6	7	5	5	4	4	3	2	3	2	3	4
27	7	8	6	6	5	5	4	3	4	3	4	5
28	8	9	7	7	6	6	5	4	5	4	5	6
29	9		8	8	7	7	5	5	6	5	6	7
30	10		9	9	8	8	6	6	6	6	7	8
31	11		10		9		7	7		7		9

Leap Years

	Jan.	Feb.	Mar.	April	May	June	July	Aug.	Sept.	Oct.	Nov.	Dec.
1	10 ♑	11 ♒	11 ♓	11 ♈	11 ♉	11 ♊	9 ♋	9 ♌	9 ♍	8 ♎	9 ♏	9 ♐
2	11	12	12	12	12	12	10	10	10	9	10	10
3	12	13	13	13	13	12	11	11	11	10	11	11
4	13	14	14	14	14	13	12	12	12	11	12	12
5	14	15	15	15	15	14	13	13	13	12	13	13
6	15	16	16	16	16	15	14	14	14	13	14	14
7	16	17	17	17	17	16	15	15	14	14	15	15
8	17	18	18	18	18	17	16	16	15	15	16	16
9	18	19	19	19	18	18	17	16	16	16	17	17
10	19	20	20	20	19	19	18	17	17	17	18	18
11	20	21	21	21	20	20	19	18	18	18	19	19
12	21	22	22	22	21	21	20	19	19	19	20	20
13	22	24	23	23	22	22	21	20	20	20	21	21
14	23	25	24	24	23	23	22	21	21	21	22	22
15	24	26	25	25	24	24	23	22	22	22	23	23
16	25	27	26	26	25	25	24	23	23	23	24	24
17	26	28	27	27	26	26	24	24	24	24	25	25
18	27	29	28	28	27	27	25	25	25	25	26	26
19	28	0 ♓	29	29	28	28	26	26	26	26	27	27
20	29	1	0 ♈	0 ♉	29	29	27	27	27	27	28	28
21	0 ♒	2	1	1	0 ♊	0 ♋	28	28	28	28	29	29
22	1	3	2	2	1	1	29	29	29	29	0 ♐	0 ♑
23	2	4	3	3	2	2	0 ♌	0 ♍	0 ♎	0 ♏	1	1
24	3	5	4	4	3	3	1	1	1	1	2	2
25	4	6	5	5	4	4	2	2	2	2	3	3
26	5	7	6	6	5	5	3	3	3	3	4	4
27	6	8	7	7	6	6	4	4	4	4	5	5
28	7	9	8	8	7	6	5	5	5	5	6	6
29	8	10	9	9	8	7	6	6	6	6	7	7
30	9		10	10	9	8	7	7	7	7	8	8
31	10		11		10		8	8		8		10

cusp; if they are *higher*, the sun goes in the House *after* that cusp.

You may find that your Sun falls directly on a cusp. If so, the Sun should be placed in the House *after* that cusp. Thus, in our example, had the Sun's position been precisely on the cusp at 22° Capricorn, we would have placed it in the First House.

To give you a complete picture, and to help you further in compiling your own birth chart, we have repeated the entire procedure to follow, shown below in a shortened version. Use this step-by-step guide for quick and easy reference, and refer to the chapter for fuller details on making each calculation.

When you have applied this process to your own birth data, you will have your own personal chart of the heavens. Now comes the exciting business of learning what your chart means and how to interpret it.

A Step-by-step Guide to Making Your Horoscope

1 Write down your date, time, and place of birth.

2 Calculate your time of birth in Star Time as follows:
(a) Find Star Time at midnight on your day of birth by looking up your birth date in Tables 1 or 2, page 111.
(b) Find out the local time of your birth.
(c) Adjust the clock time of your birth to Star Time by counting 10 seconds for each hour between midnight and the clock time of your birth.
(d) Find the Zone Time of your birth by looking up your birthplace (or the nearest large town) in Table 3, page 112.
(e) Add together the four figures you have found to give the Star Time of your birth. (If the result is higher than 24, subtract 24 from your total.)

3 Draw a map of the zodiac as a circle divided into 12 segments, representing the Houses.

4 Look up your Star Time in Table 4, pages 115–18, to find the zodiac signs and degrees to mark on your first six *cusps* or dividing lines between the Houses.

5 Insert the cusp positions you have found on your map of the zodiac, beginning at the nine o'clock position and working counterclockwise around the circle.

6 Find the zodiac signs to mark on the other six cusps by referring to the list of "opposite signs" on page 119. Remember that each of these cusps should have the opposite sign of the zodiac to the cusp immediately opposite it on your map, but is should have the same degrees.

7 Insert the positions for cusps 7 to 12 on your map.

8 Find the position of the sun in your chart as follows:
(a) Convert your local time of birth into Greenwich Mean Time.
(b) Turn to Table 5 on opposite page. If your Greenwich time of birth is *before* noon, find the sun position shown in the table for your date of birth. If your Greenwich time of birth is *after* noon, find the sun position for the day following your birth date.

9 Insert your sun position in the appropriate House on your chart, using the following method:
(a) Find the cusp sign that corresponds to the sign given for your sun position.
(b) If the number of degrees given for your sun are *lower* than those of the relevant cusp sign, put the sun in the House *before* that cusp; if they are *higher*, put the sun in the House *after* that cusp.

7

Interpreting Your Chart

Your personal chart of the zodiac is divided into 12 Houses. Each House has its own significance, and its particular meaning for each individual is indicated by the sign that "rules" it. The position of the Sun in your chart also has its own special importance. In order to interpret your chart, therefore, we need to look at each of the Houses in turn as to what they mean, how you should read them according to their ruling signs, and what the significance of the Sun's position in each House is. By putting all these elements together, you will be able to build up a complete picture from your own star chart—a unique portrait of yourself and

A horoscope is cast by following a defined procedure, which even a novice astrologer can do if he or she has the necessary data, including the meaning of the Houses. However, a horoscope is as complicated as the human personality it reflects, so that the interpretation of it becomes an art.

Right: a celestial map of about 1600, showing the magnificently intricate constellations circling around the sky in endlessly changing but eternal patterns.

"The traditional view of what the Houses mean"

of your potential for self-fulfillment, and self expression.

The general characteristics of the 12 Houses have been fairly well established since ancient times. Astrologers may today disagree about the system of House division, but almost all of them accept the traditional view of what the Houses mean. Astrologers of the Middle Ages used a simple Latin couplet to help them remember these meanings:

Vita, lucrum, fratres, genitor, nati, valetudo,
Uxor, mors, pietas, regnum, benefactaque, carcer

Which is translated into English as:

Life, money, brothers, father, children, health,
Wife, death, duty, career, benefits, prison.

These headings merely summarize the spheres of influence of the 12 Houses, and they must often be interpreted symbolically. Thus the Twelfth House can mean a real prison so that one would expect this House to be emphasized in the horoscope of a long-term convict. But the Twelfth House also stands for anything that delays and restricts a person's free will—from secret enemies to a spell of army service.

The following details will tell you more about the areas of life covered by the 12 Houses, but even these are bound to be incomplete. You will need to use your own intuitive powers to extend these attributes into every aspect of life.

First House

The personality and temperament of the *native*—the person for whom the chart is drawn. His or her physical condition, appearance, and general outlook on life. Everything about the individual that is inborn and not the product of environment.

Second House

The possessions of the native. This includes the native's ambition to succeed, as distinct from the capacity to do so. It concerns financial resources—but not money or goods obtained by inheritance.

Third House

The intellectual qualities of the native and every other faculty through which he or she expresses personality to fellow human beings. All means of communication with the world at large, and the intellectual rather than emotional relationships that the native has with close relatives, neighbors, and friends. The House also rules short casual journeys.

Fourth House

The original environment of the native—the birth place and the parental home. This includes the individual's parents and inheritance generally, but particularly from the father. It covers houses, land, and any property closely connected with the earth (for example, stock in a mining company). This House is also concerned with the conclusion of any matter, including the latter years of the native's life.

Fifth House

This House is associated with the native's sexual life and with all activities from which he or she derives particular pleasure or amusement. It therefore refers to inmost desires and to children. Gambling and speculation, as distinct from long-term investment, are also attributed to this House as long as they are undertaken in a pleasure seeking spirit.

Below: in this and all following horoscopes the Sun Sign is indicated in its House by the Symbol ☉.

ALEXANDER GRAHAM BELL

Alexander Graham Bell

Above: Bell is most famous for his invention of the telephone in 1876. Less well known is the fact that Bell's research and discoveries arose out of his own altruistic desire to teach the deaf to speak. Idealism of this kind is often characteristic of those who, like him, are born with the Sun in Pisces. Pisceans are often easy-going, which Bell certainly appears to have been.

Empress Charlotte of Mexico

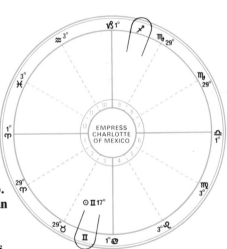

EMPRESS CHARLOTTE OF MEXICO

Left: the Empress Charlotte, also known as Carlotta, and her husband Maximilian who was the first—and last—Emperor of Mexico. In 1864 she accompanied Maximilian on his ill-fated attempt to try to establish an imperial dynasty in Mexico. Mexican and United States resistance to the plan made his position untenable, and he was executed in 1867. She suffered a mental collapse, but later made a recovery and lived in Belgium until her death in 1927. Carlotta's horoscope shows that she was born with her Sun in Gemini. What is known of her life and character demonstrates some of the best and worst aspects of the Sun-Geminians —that is, she had great personal charm combined with a perpetual restlessness and dread of boredom.

127

Annie Besant

**Above: Annie Besant, the early
social reformer, birth control
pioneer, and occultist, was born
with her Sun in Libra. However,
she was far from being the typical
Libran, and almost totally lacked
the Libran quality of moderation.
Far more influential in her makeup seems to have been Aries in the
First House. Like many Arian
types, her temperament was "commanding, choleric, and violent."**

Sixth House

The health and physical resources of the native. Everything closely connected with the individual's body, particularly food and clothing. It also refers to services that the person receives from others, to his or her employees and to any domestic pet. The House also covers any speculations undertaken purely for gain and not amusement.

Seventh House

The partners of the native, particularly the husband or wife and/or any partner in a long-lasting sexual relationship, but also including business partners. This House is also associated with legal disputes and with what astrologers used to call "open enemies"—people who frankly oppose the native's aims in life.

Eighth House

The astrologers of ancient times called this "The House of Death." They saw it as indicating the probable length of the native's life, and the way in which he or she would die. Modern astrologers tend to regard it rather as "The House of Regeneration," concerned with anything that might give new life to the individual—mentally, spiritually, or physically. All astrologers agree that legacies, wills, and other forms of inheritance come under this House.

Ninth House

The ideology of the native, his or her views on science, mysticism, and philosophy. This House describes the individual's spiritual longing and capacity to realize them. Long journeys, or travel with a serious end in view, are also attributed to this House.

Tenth House

The native's occupation and career, his or her professional status and the responsibilities and privileges it involves. The individual's relationship with superiors, whether employers or the government. This House also denotes the person's mother.

Eleventh House

This is traditionally known as "The House of Friendship." It describes the people to whom the native is naturally attracted, and the kind of relationships he or she has with them. The native's social life and general attitudes toward humanity are the concern of this House.

Twelfth House

This "House of Prison" denotes anything that interferes with the native's exercise of free will. It is the House of limitation and restraint. Such restraints may be self-imposed or may come from any number of outside factors—from interference by superiors to hostile intrigues. Secret matters generally are ruled by this House. Therefore it also denotes any secret associations—freemasonry for example—with which the native is connected. Finally, this House denotes any sphere, from prison to the army, in which discipline is the prime consideration.

The Ruling Signs in Your Chart

Each of the 12 Houses is ruled by the sign of the zodiac on its cusp—the dividing line between it and the preceding House—irrespective of any other sign which may be included in the House. In the zodiac map on page 121, for instance, the First House covers the section from the degree and sign on the first

General Gordon

Left: the murder of General Gordon in Khartoum, the Sudan, in 1885. An outstanding British soldier, Gordon has a horoscope that shows Aries 0° on the cusp of the First House of his chart, a placing which is traditionally associated with military success. Gordon was killed at the siege of Khartoum, having managed to get himself into a tactically hopeless position mainly by continually and obstinately defying his orders to withdraw. Such foolish obstinacy, often found in combination with tactlessness, is often found in Sun-Pisceans.

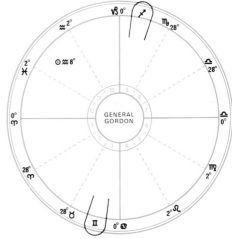

cusp (22° Capricorn) to the degree and sign on the cusp of the Second House (22° Aquarius). The First House therefore contains 22° of Aquarius. But in interpreting our map we disregard this and take the First House as being ruled by Capricorn, the Second by Aquarius, and so on.

Using the indications that follow, go through your own chart, House by House, noting down the sign that rules each one and details of the interpretations that apply in each case.

If the **First House** is ruled by
Aries: Courage, enterprise, and the ability to work hard are the main attributes of the personality. There is a notable capacity for administration, and a strong possibility that success will be achieved early in life. There is an inherent tendency to rash action which must be resisted strongly.

Isadora Duncan

Above: "Beloved Isadora," the unconventional American dancer who took Europe by storm in the years before World War I. She was born with her Sun in Gemini in the Second House. She earned big money and spent it with abandon, so it is interesting to see that this Sun's House position is supposed to indicate a tendency to extravagance, which is often balanced by good earning ability.

Taurus: The personality is friendly and cheerful. There is a love of pleasure and social life that helps to bring popularity. A tendency to be too easy-going can lead to difficulties unless it is kept firmly under control.

Gemini: The personality is quick-witted and mentally able, seeking knowledge wherever it may be found. Literature and science will be equally attractive. There is an ability to adapt to circumstance—good or bad—which will persist throughout life.

Cancer: A restless personality which may be tempered by an easy-going and comfort-loving disposition. Love of travel and change will be characteristic from youth to old age.

Leo: An ambitious and power-seeking personality which will burn for success. Generally good health and a vitality of spirit that could almost be too intense.

Virgo: The personality is a studious one, devoted to books and reading. Quick-wittedness and adaptability are the outstanding characteristics.

Libra: An amiable personality, delighting in the company of both friends and casual acquaintances. There is sometimes a tendency to be overfriendly and to place too much trust in others which can lead to trouble if not restrained.

Scorpio: At its worst, a criminal personality, seeking fulfillment of personal aims without regard for the feelings of others. However, if these tendencies are resisted, honest success can be achieved by means of a thrusting, purposeful nature and a capacity for hard work.

Sagittarius: A generous, honorable character that inspires respect. Its only drawback is a tendency to be self-righteous and priggish. Pleasurable activities often exert a great attraction, particularly those involving travel or outdoor life.

Capricorn: A persistent, self-controlled personality capable of achieving success through hard work. Practical abilities are usually combined with a shrewd mind and inner stability.

Aquarius: Independence, originality, and even eccentricity are the outstanding characteristics. There is a love of freedom and a hatred of interference which may extend to a headstrong disregard for the feelings of others. Such personalities usually have some intellectual interests and are particularly attracted by new and unusual theories.

Pisces: A strongly artistic personality often with an interest in the psychic, the mystical, and the occult. There is a tendency to be impractical and to concentrate on visions of the future rather than on the present.

If the **Second House** is ruled by:

Aries: Throughout life hard work and individual effort will be the biggest factors in earning money and acquiring wealth.

Taurus: There is some ability in handling money but also a tendency toward extravagance. In material matters much will be achieved through the goodwill of others.

Gemini: Material gain is most likely to arise from an occupation connected with communications—for example, television or journalism—or where the native acts as a go-between for other people. Some skill in the handling of money is a frequently found tendency.

Cancer: While financial affairs tend on the whole to be satisfactory, there is considerable fluctuation in fortune. This is sometimes combined with extravagance and a love of rich living.

Leo: There is an ability to acquire money easily. Unfortunately this is often accompanied by gross extravagance.

Virgo: Occupations involved with communication are most likely to prove profitable. Good at handling money and conducting financial affairs in general.

Libra: Extravagance and financial skill fight for supremacy. The help of friends is often financially advantageous.

Scorpio: Financial success can be achieved through a combination of industriousness and adventurousness.

Sagittarius: A talent for financial matters and the accumulation of personal wealth are frequent tendencies.

Capricorn: Financial ability combined with carefulness result in a slow but steady accumulation of material possessions.

Aquarius: Extravagance is likely to imperil financial stability. There is a risk of unexpected losses, possibly arising from the native's own restlessness.

Pisces: A love of luxury and imprudence with money endanger happiness, as does the possibility of losing money through fraud.

Angela Davis

Left: with her undoubtedly sincere concern for those whom she believes to be oppressed, Angela Davis demonstrates the characteristics of a certain type of Sun-Aquarian. Such Aquarians are often, like Angela Davis, deeply involved in political or humanitarian causes. For her, as for all strongly Aquarian personalities, a career is a vocation rather than just a means of making money. Her belief in a total equality between the sexes is also typical of the Aquarian type of woman.

131

Greta Garbo

Right: Greta Garbo, the world-famous film star, was born with her Sun in the sign of Virgo, and is in fact a typical Virgoan. Despite her undoubted charm and sex appeal she, like all strongly Virgoan women, has found that mere femininity is not enough for her. She has not wanted to confine herself to the exploitation of her womanhood, but rather to perform a task in life—and to do it well. Also typically Virgoan is Greta Garbo's lifelong preference for genuine criticism of her artistic achievement rather than journalistic flattery that concentrates on her beauty as a woman—a preference she now expresses by her shunning of all publicity during her extended and intensely private retirement.

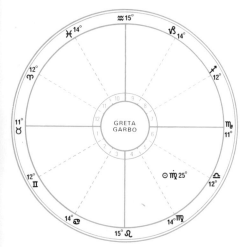

If the **Third House** is ruled by:

Aries: Alertness and drive can lead to early success, but the native must learn to control his or her argumentativeness.

Taurus: There is a marked interest in literature and the arts and a notably happy disposition.

Gemini: Intellectual faculties are good, and a full use of these combined with adaptability and practicality are likely to lead to a successful life.

Cancer: The individual will do well and be thoroughly happy as long as life involves a certain amount of travel and change.

Leo: A keen mind leads to an expansive and pleasant existence.

Virgo: The native is happiest if life involves travel and/or the handling of money.

Libra: Life will be particularly happy if it involves travel or the arts.

Scorpio: Energy and hard work bring a happy and successful life.

Sagittarius: An optimistic and good-tempered individual who will prove popular with others.

Capricorn: A serious mind, not always good at communicating, but capable of concentration and getting to the heart of matters.

Aquarius: This individual has good mental and intuitive abilities combined with a tendency to eccentricity. A lover of travel and all things new.

Pisces: A person who thoroughly enjoys traveling and communicating with others. A tendency to gloom is sometimes present and needs to be controlled.

If the **Fourth House** is ruled by:

Aries: The rewards of personal effort may be supplemented by gains from inheritance or marriage. Throughout life there will be the temptation and the opportunity to engage in domestic quarrels.

Taurus: The native will care intensely for attractive home surroundings. Home life can, and probably will, contribute much to personal happiness.

Gemini: The home and home conditions are likely to dominate the native's mind to an unhealthy degree.

Cancer: Family life, whether with parents or marriage partner, is always of great importance. Frequent moving may occur. There is some possibility of gain from trading in houses or land.

Leo: Family ties are strong and there is a possibility of inheritance from the father.

Virgo: Too much concentration on domestic matters can lead to neurosis.

Libra: Home life is of major importance and does much to enrich the personality.

Scorpio: A tendency to quarrel can disrupt home life unless strictly controlled. There may be gains by inheritance.

Sagittarius: Home life is of great importance. There is a possibility of gain from trading in land, houses, or other possessions connected with the earth.

Capricorn: Home life tends to give rise to cares and difficulties.

Aquarius: Frequent changes of home are likely, and there may be a tendency to adopt an unconventional way of life.

Pisces: Home life tends to be harmonious and family links strong.

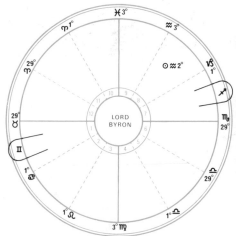

Lord Byron

Left: "Mad, bad Lord Byron," the club-footed Romantic poet whose amorous exploits scandalized English society until his death in 1824, when he gave his life for the cause of Greek independence. Byron was born with the Sun in Aquarius. His life and character show in many ways the marks of that unconventional sign. Personal freedom and the determination to overcome everything that opposes it is the highest aim of the strongly Aquarian personality. Hardly any Aquarian ever displayed these characteristics more blatantly than Byron, whose defiance of convention even ran to his having an affair with his own half-sister.

J. P. Morgan

Above: in Morgan's horoscope, shown below, the rulership by Leo of the First House suggested that this swashbuckling 19th-century multimillionaire would prove ambitious, power-seeking, eager for success. Moreover, the Virgo rulership of the Second House suggests that he would be "good at handling money and financial affairs conducting in general." In fact, he was the master of Wall Street of his period. Morgan's Sun was in Aries, which indicates that he was a pioneering, adventuring type who always took the lead.

If the **Fifth House** is ruled by:

Aries: The native will have a strong interest in the opposite sex—an interest mingled with a desire for domination.

Taurus: Sexuality and all pleasurable activities will be a strong center of interest.

Gemini: A rather refined attitude to sex—technique not passion being noticeable in close personal relationships.

Cancer: Sexual attachments tend to be short lived. A somewhat fickle attitude toward the opposite sex is sometimes displayed.

Leo: Sexual drives are strong but not all-powerful. Charm of personality is often a strong element in attracting members of the opposite sex to the native.

Virgo: A tendency to act, rather than to feel genuine emotion in sexual relationships.

Libra: Pleasure, including sexual pleasure, is often of great importance for the native's happiness in life.

Scorpio: A powerful sexual drive is allied with a desire to be the dominant partner in all relationships, whatever their nature.

Sagittarius: Sexual and social success is likely throughout life. This success may not only bring pleasure but also result in material gain.

Capricorn: The sexual drive is not usually strong. Gambling or other kind of speculation will often be successful if it is for pleasure alone.

Aquarius: Attitudes toward sexual relationships will tend to be unconventional.

Pisces: Love of luxury is likely to be allied with great indulgence in sexual and other pleasurable activities.

If the **Sixth House** is ruled by:

Aries: Health is likely to be good. The native will prosper as the member of a large organization.

Taurus: Health will probably be good. The native will be able to achieve success through his or her harmonious relationships with others.

Gemini: There is a tendency to overtax both physical and mental resources, and this should be controlled.

Cancer: Service to others will lead to success in life.

Leo: There is a marked ability to take responsibility and a tendency to change occupation frequently.

Virgo: Worry, excessive mental activity, and a tendency to over-tax the body are the main dangers to health.

Libra: Health, both physical and mental, is likely to be good.

Scorpio: Health is generally good. There are great reserves of physical and mental energy.

Sagittarius: Health is usually excellent. The general psychological makeup of the native inspires respect and calls forth cooperation from others.

Capricorn: Health is sound and there is a probability of long life. Emotions are controlled and disciplined.

Aquarius: A highly strung temperament. A tendency to excessive irritability must be controlled if psychological ill health is to be avoided.

Pisces: There is a strong tendency to introversion and a love of solitude.

If the **Seventh House** is ruled by:

Aries: There is a tendency to marry early in life. The chosen partner is often a person of strong, even dominating, character.

Taurus: Marriage or other romantic partnerships tend to play an important part in life.

Gemini: Marriage and partnership generally are likely to play an important part in the native's occupation.

Cancer: Marriage and partnerships are both likely to prove financially advantageous.

Leo: Marriage and partnership play a major role in life and may well bring a rise in social status.

Virgo: Marriage or romantic partnership may well be with a younger person.

Libra: Marriage and romance play an exceptionally important part in life.

Scorpio: A certain quality of impetuousness may well lead to unusual domestic circumstances.

Sagittarius: Marriage and partnerships are likely to bring great material benefits.

Capricorn: Marriage may well be delayed until late in life. When it comes it should bring great happiness.

Aquarius: A quality of inconstancy can, if not mastered, lead to difficulties in marriage and partnerships.

Pisces: Fickleness is a threat to relationships. If this is guarded against, marriage and partnerships should prove happy.

If the **Eighth House** is ruled by:

Aries: Some financial gain is likely to come from legacies or partnerships.

Taurus: Marriage and partnership will probably be of major importance materially, producing either great gains or losses.

Gemini: Financial gain is likely through partnerships.

Cancer: There is a possibility that money will be acquired from the native's marriage partner or mother.

Leo: There is a possibility of financial benefit through marriage.

Virgo: A partnership involving literature or science is the most likely source of gain.

Libra: Partnership, marriage, and legacies will have a major financial impact—sometimes good, and sometimes bad.

Scorpio: Financial gain is probable from marriage or inheritance.

Sagittarius: Financial gains from marriage and inheritance are likely.

Capricorn: Major financial gains are likely to come from hard work rather than marriage or inheritance. The span of life should be long.

Aquarius: Sudden and unexpected gains are a possibility.

Pisces: Financial affairs are always liable to fluctuation.

If the **Ninth House** is ruled by:

Aries: A marked love of change and a certain argumentativeness are strong characteristics.

Taurus: A charming personality with a strong artistic bent.

Gemini: Travel is likely to be an important source of pleasure.

Cancer: An imaginative personality whose opinions are liable to sudden change.

Charles Baudelaire

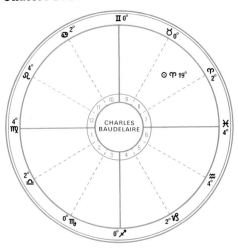

Below: Baudelaire—drug taker, Satanist, close to madness yet one of France's greatest 19th-century poets—ended his life in a mental asylum. Several features in his astrological make-up made such an end a likely one. The rulership of the Sixth House by Aquarius is taken by many to show a highly strung temperament that must at all costs avoid a way of life that could lead to psychological ill health. With his drug taking, his hectic love life, and his other extravagances, Baudelaire courted his tragic fate.

John Lennon

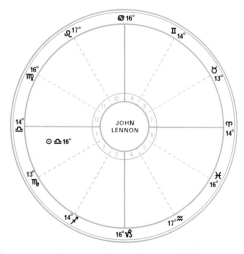

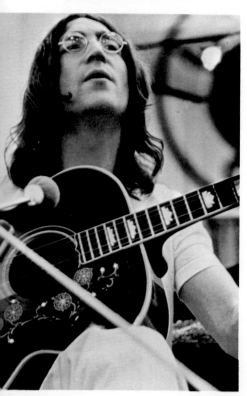

Below: John Lennon, perhaps the most famous of all the Beatles and one who continues a noteworthy career in his own right, was born with the Sun in the First House of his chart, a position traditionally associated with a personality that is ambitious and eager for fame and power. The Libra rulership of the First House and the Sun's position in the same sign also suggest an amiable and pleasant character.

Leo: An ambitious and idealistic personality inclined to intellectual pursuits.
Virgo: Occupation may be linked with travel which will, in any case, be an important factor in life.
Libra: An idealistic, sensitive, artistic, and generous personality.
Scorpio: A mentally alert personality with a love of change and a tendency to quarrelsomeness.
Sagittarius: A tolerant, kind-hearted, and philosophical personality.
Capricorn: A personality that holds strongly to its opinions.
Aquarius: Unconventional ways of thought can lead to a certain fanaticism.
Pisces: An imaginative, intuitive, and beauty-loving personality.

If the **Tenth House** is ruled by:
Aries: An ambitious and masterful temperament which can lead to great success.
Taurus: Success is most likely to be achieved through the good will of superiors.
Gemini: Business ability and mental alertness can lead to early success in occupations.
Cancer: Occupations connected with the public at large are most likely to lead to popularity and success.
Leo: An ability to hold positions of some prominence should be exploited for the achievement of success.
Virgo: A capacity for self-expression and a marked business ability make success highly probable.
Libra: Popularity, especially with superiors and people of the opposite sex, can lead to success.
Scorpio: Ambition, executive ability, and a certain ruthlessness can bring success.
Sagittarius: The native's occupation is likely to bring prestige and financial prosperity.
Capricorn: Self-reliance, hard work, and ambition can lead to success, though sometimes not until late in life.
Aquarius: Hatred of restrictions and an undue love of change often prevent success from being achieved.
Pisces: The achievement of success in an occupation depends on whether ambition or irresponsibility is most prominent in the makeup of the personality.

If the **Eleventh House** is ruled by:
Aries: The essential energy of the native's social life usually ensures many friends.
Taurus: Friendship is of great importance and friends are many.
Gemini: Friends are plentiful if the native can control a tendency to indulge in too much criticism of others.
Cancer: A wide range of friends, many of whom will be women, whatever the sex of the native.
Leo: Friends can contribute much to success in every sphere of life.
Virgo: Many friends can be acquired through travel and active participation in clubs and societies.
Libra: A great many friends make friendship a major factor in the life of the native.

Mahatma Gandhi

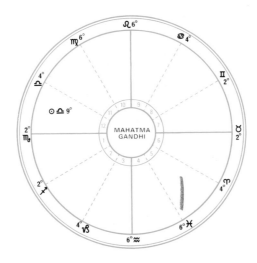

Right: this remarkable man, the architect of India's independence through his own brand of nonviolent revolution, has his Sun in the Twelfth House. This suggests he would both be a lover of solitude and be likely to suffer family disagreements. In fact, Gandhi spent long hours in quiet meditation, and was estranged from his son.

Scorpio: Energy in social affairs brings friends who must not be alienated by any temptation to exploit their friendship.
Sagittarius: A popular personality whose friends help in the achievement of the native's desires.
Capricorn: Friends are not many in number, but they are extremely loyal.
Aquarius: Friends are most likely to be found among people of unconventional views.
Pisces: A wide circle of friends, some of whom may prove inconstant or even false.

If the **Twelfth House** is ruled by:
Aries: Strong administrative ability often brings success in spite of obstacles.
Taurus: The personality will be at its best away from the public eye.
Gemini: Worry can be a major obstacle to success, and must be avoided to achieve success.
Cancer: The native should avoid too much public prominence.
Leo: There is always some possibility of conflict with those in authority.
Virgo: A tendency to be too concerned with petty matters can be an obstacle to success.
Libra: Some element of seclusion in life makes for happiness.
Scorpio: Powerful abilities can overcome obstacles.
Sagittarius: Willingness to help others means that they, in turn, help the native to overcome obstacles.
Capricorn: A certain desire for solitude is likely.
Aquarius: Sudden and unexpected misfortunes sometimes stand in the native's way.
Pisces: A love of seclusion is combined with a taste for clandestine friendships.

137

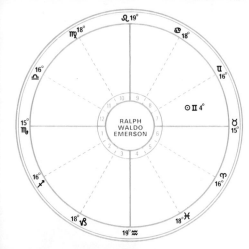

Ralph Waldo Emerson

Below left: Emerson, the New England poet, essayist, and philosopher, had his Sun in Gemini, traditionally the patron sign of intellectuals. His Sun was in the Seventh House, which shows that he was capable of enjoying a happy and emotionally satisfying marriage, which he did in fact have. Emerson's Ninth House was ruled by Cancer, suggesting a tendency to change one's opinions—and Emerson frequently reconsidered his judgments. For example, he once believed that all philosophers should do some manual labor, but later said that "intellectuals should not dig."

By now you should have noted down the interpretations of the 12 zodiac signs that rule the Houses in your map. Next you should make a similar note of the significance of the Sun's position in the zodiac, which you can obtain from the 12 Sun Sign outlines contained in Chapter 3. If, for instance, your Sun is in Libra, look up the description of the Libran personality in Chapter 3.

Finally, you need to check the meaning of the Sun's House position from the following list.

Sun in First House: An ambitious, even power-loving, personality blessed with good physical health.

Sun in Second House: An extravagant personality is balanced by a capacity to earn money easily.

Sun in Third House: A somewhat intellectual personality with a keen interest in science and literature.

Sun in Fourth House: A family-minded individual with a gift for managing property and land.

Sun in Fifth House: A sociable personality strongly interested in music, drama, and the opposite sex.

Sun in Sixth House: A capacity for administration can lead to an extremely successful life.

Sun in Seventh House: A personality to whom marriage is both important and socially advantageous.

Sun in Eighth House: A financially lucky individual who may obtain wealth through marriage or inheritance.

Sun in Ninth House: An intellectual, ambitious, and travel-loving personality.

Sun in Tenth House: An ability to take responsibility will lead to favors from those in authority.

Sun in Eleventh House: Friends may well help this individual toward the fulfillment of ambitions and desires.

Sun in Twelfth House: A lover of solitude tending to have disagreements with relatives.

You now have 14 pieces of information on which to make your overall judgment of the map—the 12 interpretations of the zodiac signs that rule the Houses, the meaning of the Sun's position in the zodiac, and the significance of the Sun's position in each House. All that remains is to blend these 14 indications into a composite portrait.

Some people find this process easy; for others it is extremely difficult. It is a knack that you have to acquire for yourself, using

Louis Pasteur

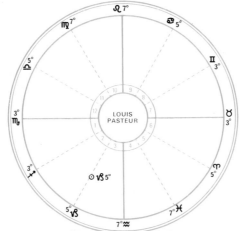

Right: Pasteur, the great 19th-century French chemist and microbiologist who firmly established the germ theory of disease, had his Sun in the Third House. This strongly suggested that he would prove to be an intellectual with a particular interest in science. The Sun was in Capricon, a position associated with a passion for detail and precision. Pasteur clearly showed this characteristic in his painstaking experiments.

Mary Baker Eddy

**Above: the founder of Christian
Science was born with her Sun
in Cancer, which is above all the
sign of motherliness. Certainly
this remarkable woman became a
mother to the thousands of faithful followers she gained in her
lifetime. In fact, many of her
close adherents referred to her as
"Mother." Her husbands—she
had three—were weak-willed,
unstable personalities, the type
of man, in fact, to which Cancerian
women are often attracted.**

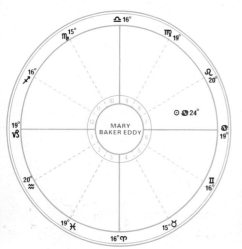

a combination of intuition and practice. Nevertheless, a few hints can help you learn how to blend the various elements into a successful reading of your map.

Firstly, do not reject your chart out of hand because some of the indications seem to contradict each other, or because some of them do not appear to fit your personality—or that of the person for whom you may have prepared the map. The contradictory factors may well exist in you or the individual concerned, but may either be totally repressed or only apparent in times of stress.

For example, suppose most of the 14 factors indicate an extremely sociable and popular personality. The Sun, however, is in the Twelfth House, which indicates a love of solitude. This would probably be an individual who is normally extremely fond of company, but who wishes to be alone at times.

Again, say that one House showed a capacity to manage money well while another showed a tendency to extravagance. We could expect the behavior pattern of the person concerned to fluctuate, probably cyclically, between the two extremes.

The second thing to remember when blending your interpretations is that you can apply the brief interpretation given for the ruling sign of each House to any of the various aspects of life covered by that House. These are listed earlier in the chapter under the meanings of the Twelve Houses.

On this basis, if the Tenth House is ruled by Aquarius the interpretation given is: "Hatred of restrictions and an undue love of change often prevent success from being achieved." However, as you can see from the list of House meanings, the Tenth House refers among other things to the mother of the native. Therefore two interpretations can be extended to the mother: firstly, the mother may tend to hold unorthodox and changeable opinions; secondly, she may have strained relationships with her children.

The final method to use in making your overall interpretation of the map is to write a short character sketch. Do this even if you have prepared the chart for yourself, in which case it can help to imagine that you are describing someone else. Take all 14 interpretations as representing various facets of this one particular person. Then try to produce a composite portrait of the person in which all the factors, even those that may at first sight appear contradictory, are combined to form a unified whole.

This is a technique that comes more easily with practice—and you may be surprised at some of the insights you gain into your character or that of your friends. If you are tempted to go deeper into astrology by drawing up maps for other people, you will gradually develop your skill at interpreting your findings.

One thing is certain. Your experience in drawing up and interpreting your own star chart will have told you a great deal more about how astrology and astrologers work. Modern astrologers are wary of predicting events. They believe that astrology's greatest practical value lies in the diagnosis of a person's character, and the assessment of his or her potentialities. Whatever the heavens may indicate about a person's destiny, astrologers believe that their particular brand of insight can offer people fuller and happier lives through a deeper understanding of themselves and others, and a greater awareness of mankind's place as an integral part of the Universe.

Bobby Fischer

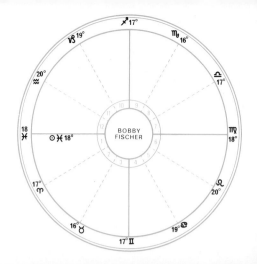

Below: Fischer has his Sun in Pisces, and Sun-Pisceans are often "amiable, vague, and sometimes devious"—an excellent description of this outstanding chess player and his relationship both with his opponents and with some of those who have promoted his matches. Since no exact time of birth is available, this is a solar chart with the Sun on the cusp of the First House, but it is still interesting to notice that his Tenth House is ruled by Sagittarius, which would suggest that Fischer's occupation is likely to bring him both fame and prosperity—as it surely has.

Astrology Today

The interest in astrology today in both the United States and Europe is more widespread than at any time since the 17th century. The signs of the zodiac are household words, and almost every one of us knows our Sun Sign and the general characteristics of those born under that sign. There are thousands of popular newspaper and magazine horoscope columns as well as the occasional foray of television into the subject. More important perhaps are the significant, if limited, scientific studies that have been undertaken in recent years. Does this mean that a uniform and codified theory of the cosmic influence is likely to be accepted into the general body of scientific beliefs in our day? Or is the current boom in astrology merely a reflection of the troubled times in which we live? Will the idea that the heavenly bodies influence human life again sink into forgotten lore if the future of mankind becomes more secure?

There are certain people today who say that astrology has no place in modern life, that it is simply one of the occult fads that deserve to die out as fads do. On the other hand, some of the very people who have traditionally been most critical and skeptical of astrology—the scientists—are providing evidence that suggests astrology may be founded on fact. The research of radio engineer John H. Nelson in the United States, for example, showed an unmistakable link between radio static and the position of the planets. Dr. Leonard Ravitz, a professor at Duke University in North Carolina, has seemed to prove the age-old folk belief that the full Moon increases mental disturbance. American psychologist Vernon Clark and French statistician Michel Gauquelin have demonstrated that techniques of astrology can be shown to work when subjected to tough statistical investigation. The research of such down-to-earth scientists cannot so easily be dismissed as head-in-the-clouds conjecture.

The International Society for Astrological Research, Inc. (ISAR), with headquarters in Ohio, also speaks for the respectability of astrology. Founded in 1968, it numbers some of the world's most famous and serious astrologers among its members. They stand united in the aim to regain for astrology "its position in the academic and scientific field." They use computers and other modern aids in the research projects they sponsor, which have ranged from a study of the possibility of predicting earthquakes by cosmic signs to an investigation into the influence of cosmic bodies on poor spelling ability.

But could astrology ever be a real science in the dictionary definition of the word? Many modern practitioners who answered a questionnaire compiled by Marcia Moore in 1959 for a thesis accepted by Harvard University indicated at least a scientific approach. Moreover, almost 80 percent of her respondents identified astrology as a science in the sense of developing "more knowledge of the operations of natural law as it works through man, the world, and the cosmos." One reply went so far as to say that astrologers should study mathematical logic and discipline themselves to use scientific methods.

Nevertheless some modern astrologers continue to hold that their art can never be separated from the occult, that it is in its essence occult. R. H. Naylor, one of the best-known 20th-century astrologists, always warned students starting the study of astrology not to treat the subject as occult. However, he himself admitted that "the advanced study of the subject must necessarily lead you and me into that elusive twilight that lies between known and unknown; the seen and the unseen." This seeming contradiction may be what keeps the skeptics so skeptical.

Dane Rudhyar, author of *The Astrology of Personality*, seems to be on another tack in defending astrology's place in modern life. He fully accepts it as a system of thought while maintaining that it is different from a science. In fact, he insists that reliance on scientific method and criterions would "denature astrology." However, his complex and difficult-to-follow reasoning about the development of a new "cosmobiology" applying to "the whole biosphere" departs from most practicing astrologers' beliefs.

Lyall Watson, author of the sensational best seller *Supernature* and a scientist himself, feels that science and astrology now have far more in common than either skeptics or supporters realize. He is convinced that astrology has a hard core of truth. "The cosmos is a chaotic frenzy of wave patterns," he says, "some of which have been orchestrated on Earth into an organized life system. The harmony between the two can be understood only with the aid of a score, and of all the possibilities open to us at this moment, astrology (for all its weird origins and sometimes even weirder devotees) seems to offer the best interpretation."

Whatever the result of future scientific investigation—and there are voices like that of Derek Parker who in *Astrology in the Modern World* calls for fuller examination still—it is the desire to understand how human beings fit into the scheme of things that is likely to insure astrology's survival in the modern West as in the East. For in a culture that is marked by change and upheaval, by wars and social and political revolutions, by increasing mental illness and nervous disorders, astrology provides something that is notably missing in everyday life: pattern, rhythm, and order.

This is the function of astrology that attracted many great thinkers of the past like Plato, Ptolemy, Johannes Kepler, and Isaac Newton. This is what continues to attract people to astrology more than to any other unorthodox theory of cosmic influence on daily life.

Genuine astrology has little to do with the generalized predictions of newspaper horoscopes. It is rather a means of helping human beings to discover more about their own essential personalities, and to understand their relationship to their Universe. In no age has such understanding been more important.

Picture Credits